Australian career coach Kate James helps her clients to find direction and build self-belief. Kate works with individual clients, facilitates confidence workshops online and hosts retreats for women in Melbourne and Byron Bay. She continues her own studies into positive psychology, Acceptance and Commitment Therapy (ACT), mindfulness and self-compassion and is the author of five books, *Change Your Thinking to Change Your Life*, *Believe in Yourself*, *Be Mindful*, *Change How You Think* and *Create Calm*.

Also by Kate James

Change Your Thinking to Change Your Life

Quietly Confident

An introvert's guide to knowing
and expressing your worth

KATE JAMES

MACMILLAN
Pan Macmillan Australia

Pan Macmillan acknowledges the Traditional Custodians of Country throughout Australia and their connections to lands, waters and communities. We pay our respect to Elders past and present and extend that respect to all Aboriginal and Torres Strait Islander peoples today. We honour more than sixty thousand years of storytelling, art and culture.

Some of the people in this book have had their names changed to protect their identities.

First published 2024 in Macmillan by Pan Macmillan Australia Pty Ltd
1 Market Street, Sydney, New South Wales, Australia, 2000

A catalogue record for this book is available from the National Library of Australia

NATIONAL LIBRARY OF AUSTRALIA

Typeset in 12.5/18 pt Adobe Garamond Pro by Midland Typesetters, Australia

Printed by IVE
Illustration on page 110 © The Studio/Shutterstock

We advise that the information contained in this book does not negate personal responsibility on the part of the reader for their own health and safety. It is recommended that individually tailored advice is sought from your healthcare or medical professional. The publishers and their respective employees, agents and authors, are not liable for injuries or damage occasioned to any person as a result of reading or following the information contained in this book.

The author and the publisher have made every effort to contact copyright holders for material used in this book. Any person or organisation that may have been overlooked should contact the publisher.

MIX
Paper from responsible sources
FSC® C018183
www.fsc.org

The paper in this book is FSC® certified. FSC® promotes environmentally responsible, socially beneficial and economically viable management of the world's forests.

For my wise and courageous daughters, Elsa and Meg,
who have taught me the most about confidence.

Contents

Part One Meaning

Part Two Connection

Quietly Confident

Introduction

Introverts in an extroverted world

'I'm so frustrated with myself,' says Clare, shifting in her seat and lowering her gaze. 'It's the same thing every month. I promise myself the next meeting will be different and then I'm sitting in that board room again listening to everyone say their piece while I clam up and nod along. Then the meeting is over, and I haven't contributed, in any way . . .' She's on the verge of tears, and I understand why she's frustrated: a pattern she's been trying to break for a long time has repeated yet again, crushing her self-esteem.

Clare has worked in the same non-profit organisation for six years, is intelligent, knowledgeable and respected by her peers, yet she hesitates to contribute when in group settings. Often, when she does find the courage to speak up, one of her more confident colleagues talks over her.

Like many of my clients, Clare is an introvert, and in a business setting, her natural style of communication seems to work

1

against her. This is evidenced by the fact that she's been over-looked for promotion on more than one occasion. For most of her life, Clare has wrestled with the idea that she needs to change in order to fit in. At the same time, she knows instinctively that if she wants to be genuinely happy, she needs to be true to herself.

Raised in a family of introverts, Clare grew up being told not to be too loud, dominating or overly ambitious. At school she was praised for her quiet conscientiousness and kindness and, as a result, she's spent her life believing that being 'nice' is more important than pushing her own agenda. As an adult, however, Clare has been given conflicting advice.

Clare knows she's different to her more outspoken colleagues by nature. She's calm, thoughtful and more interested in living a harmonious life than aspiring to wealth or power. At the same time, she feels she has much to offer at her workplace. Clare doesn't always know how to unlock her courage and potential or express a quiet confidence that aligns with her values, and she feels unsure about how to operate effectively while being the best possible version of herself in this world. For these reasons, she's enlisted my help.

Often, introverts like Clare can feel like something of a contradiction. While she may not want to spend every weekend at a party, she at least wants to be invited. Even though she enjoys time on her own and needs it to recharge, she loves the company of like-minded people. And sometimes in a group environment, she feels lonelier than when she's on her own. Clare's challenge is finding a way to reconcile the conflicting aspects of herself while also remaining authentic.

The specifics of Clare's situation are unique, but I've heard variations on these themes for over two decades from intelligent and talented people who doubt themselves in some way. The people I coach are mostly sensitive introverts – primarily women but occasionally men – struggling to live in a way that is 'confident'. Many of them are self-described perfectionists, more than three-quarters say they feel like an imposter in certain areas of their lives, and almost all acknowledge that a lack of confidence is holding them back in some way. Some fear they are falling short at work, others are seeking help with their relationships, but a common denominator is that all of them have an unmet desire to build a genuine and enduring sense of self-belief.

$\sim$

If you close your eyes and picture someone confident, chances are you'll envisage someone who's relaxed and outgoing, or perhaps courageous and risk-taking. The kind of person who walks into a room in an open and self-assured way. Someone who can hold court at a party or 'work the room' at a networking event. They hold eye contact with ease, don't shy away from conflict or a direct conversation, and seem completely comfortable in their own skin. It's also likely, given you're reading this book, that this may not be how you see yourself. And maybe you're not even sure it's how you want to be.

The version of confidence we've come to recognise in Western culture is what Susan Cain, the bestselling author of *Quiet*, calls the 'extrovert ideal'. We've been conditioned to aspire to it because it garners attention, respect, promotions and first dates. It's this type of confidence that the introverts I work with often feel they should emulate, although intuitively, many question if they really want it. They frequently sense that even if it was what they aspired to, an extroverted style of confidence is probably not attainable for them because it plays to the natural strengths of those with extroverted personalities.

In 1921, Swiss psychiatrist Carl Jung identified two attitude types that sit on either end of a spectrum: reflective, contemplative introverts at one end, and outgoing, energetic extroverts at the other. In recent years, 'ambivert' has been added to the mix to describe someone with both introverted *and* extroverted traits.

Each personality type has its own set of strengths and weaknesses, and neither type is 'better' or 'worse' than the other. While extroverts draw their energy from their external interactions, introverts draw energy from within. Introverts have a rich inner world, and they rely heavily on their thoughts and feelings. They're content to spend time alone (and need it to recharge), but they still need and enjoy other people. Their preference is for one-to-one interactions with like-minded people. Extroverts, on the other hand, are more socially active, feel energised from time spent with others, enjoy being part of groups and prefer less time alone.

Introverts make up as much as 30 to 50 per cent of the world's population, a statistic that surprises many people. Maybe this is because introverts are often painted as the *exception* to the norm – rare, antisocial wallflowers in a garden of extroverted butterflies – rather than what we truly are: another equally valuable version of normal.

Somewhere along the way, the stereotype of the confident, social extrovert became fused with the Western ideal of what a

charismatic and decisive leader should be, and even what constitutes a successful 'average' person. Introverts have often paid the
price for society's glorification of Cain's 'extrovert ideal', but with
greater awareness and celebration of their gifts, it's my hope that
books like hers and this one will help to redress the balance.

ONE

What would you do if you were *really* confident?

Take a moment to think about what it was that compelled you to pick up this book. When you started toying with the idea of building your confidence, did you have a specific area of your life in mind? Is there a long-held dream you've put on hold because you don't believe you'll be able to achieve it? Does your lack of confidence stop you from speaking up in meetings or asking for what you need? Maybe, like me, your desire for more confidence is about gaining a deeper understanding of yourself, a greater sense of self-acceptance and ultimately, a stronger sense of self-worth across all areas of your life.

Regardless of why you've chosen this book, you may find completing the following two exercises helpful before you get any further into the content.

What would you change?

1. Grab a couple of blank sheets of paper and using 'stream of consciousness writing' (which really just means, write quickly and don't edit), spend around ten minutes writing out a description of how you imagine the most confident version of yourself, including what you would do if you were truly confident. The most effective way to do this is to write in the present tense and be a bit creative. Include anything you'd love to achieve in your life.

2. Reflect on the following areas and consider which are immediately of interest to you. Choose as many areas as you like from the long list below or use these examples as inspiration to identify your own areas to work on. Once you have done this, I recommend prioritising three or four to focus on as you work your way through the rest of the book. In Part One: Meaning, we'll talk about setting specific goals, and the areas you identify here will help you with that exercise.

Self-belief

Trust my intuition

Be true to myself

Stay calm under pressure

Regulate my emotions

Stop self-sabotaging

See my goals through to the end

Be better at decision-making

Give up perfectionism

Forgive myself for my past mistakes

Find the courage to take risks

Stop comparing myself to other people

Be kinder to myself

Celebrate my wins (including the small ones)

Relationships

Feel comfortable to set boundaries

Be confident to ask for what I want

Speak up when I have a concern

Be more open and vulnerable

Feel confident to be able to admit when I'm wrong

Be a role model for others

Stop people-pleasing

Social

Feel confident to make new friends

Ask someone on a date (or accept an invitation)

Become more confident to be intimate

Be proactive in organising social functions

Career

Speak up when there are challenges at work

Ask for my workload to be varied or changed

Leave my current role and find something that's a better fit

Apply for a role where I don't meet all of the selection criteria

Apply for a more senior role

Speak up more regularly in meetings

Feel confident in public speaking

Have the confidence to share my work with others

Sell myself in an interview

Feel confident with my resume and LinkedIn profile

Engage my strengths more often

Let go of imposter syndrome

Health
Commit to a regular habit of exercise
Practise self-care
Proactively make appointments with medical professionals

Creativity
Make time for my creative practice
Share my creative work with others
Feel brave enough to dance/sing/play music/make art/be
    creative – simply for the joy of it

Physical appearance
Accept my body exactly as it is (including any of my perceived flaws)
Stop using my physical appearance as an excuse not to do things
Value myself enough to take care of my physical appearance
Dress confidently, in my own style

Living environment
Create a home that feels nurturing and comfortable
Decorate my home in a style that feels like 'me'

Advocacy
Speak up on behalf of people who aren't able to advocate for
    themselves
Feel confident to share my genuine opinions
Get behind causes that matter to me

Financial
Manage my personal finances well
Feel confident to ask for my salary to be reviewed
Create a long-term personal financial plan

Spiritual
Have my own spiritual beliefs
Believe in something bigger than myself

Joy

Be a more positive person

Embrace lightness and joy in my life (without feeling like it's
    embarrassing or silly)

Laugh more and be willing to share humour

Your dreams

Pursue my version of an ideal life

Trust myself to take action in the direction of my dreams

Have faith that I'll be okay with whatever happens

The 'confidence equals competence' myth

How many of us find ourselves deferring to the person with the loudest opinions because we assume that if they're dominating the conversation, they must know what they're talking about? As it turns out, bold assertions are not accurate predictors of a person's ability.

In 1999, social psychologists David Dunning and Justin Kruger confirmed what many had long suspected: that an individual's confidence is not an accurate indicator of their competence – and often the gap between confidence and competence is significant.

Their original study involved testing people on grammar, humour and logic, and they found that those who scored the lowest also tended to overestimate (quite dramatically) how well they'd performed. Many put themselves in the 62nd percentile when their actual scores placed them in the 12th percentile. Paradoxically, people with more expertise tend to feel less confident, primarily because they recognise how little they know and how much more knowledge there is to be gained.

This phenomenon of having overconfidence in an ability or skill without the competence to back it up was named the Dunning–Kruger effect, and though the original study focused on those with low competence, the effect isn't limited to people with low IQs. It also plays out when someone knows a little about a certain topic yet speaks about it as though they're an expert; or when they overestimate their skills in a sport they haven't played in a long time (and maybe weren't that great at in the first place); or when a person believes themselves to be more charismatic, interesting or funny than they really are.

It's likely that you know someone like this. Maybe a colleague who emphatically states that the marketing campaign they prefer is superior to all others, or a member of your book club who 'knows' exactly what the author intended, shutting down everyone else's comments, or the person who dominates the conversation at a dinner party, confidently sharing opinions about current world events with only a moderate degree of accuracy. It's also likely that even if you are across the true facts yourself, you hesitate to chime in because you don't want to be the kind of person who corrects others or draws attention to themselves.

The cost of low confidence

In my experience, introverts are more likely than extroverts to believe that certain areas of life are off limits to them. They might see something they want to pursue, but think, *I'm not the kind of person who [gets the guy/girl, earns that salary, wins those awards, can entertain people with anecdotes at a party]*. They see certain things as being reserved for someone who fits their idea of what a confident person looks like (i.e., not them).

Confidence has often been described as 'life's enabler' and research strongly supports this description, demonstrating that success is more closely related to confidence than it is to competence. The implications of not having enough confidence extend into every facet of life, and not just for our species. In nature, animals that display stereotypically confident traits and 'alpha' qualities are the ones that dominate. The more assertive and powerful they are, the faster they rise to the top of the pack. The strongest and most assertive will assume the highest spot in the hierarchy of their group – allowing them to eat first, take their pick of mates and enjoy prime territory. This is true whether we're talking about seals, chimps, wolves, lions, meerkats or humans. It's also the case in corporate America where extroverted alpha males represent 70 per cent of the country's CEOs.

Not everyone aspires to alpha-like levels, however. Most of us are happy to stay a little more in the background but we also want to feel that when it's called for (or when we want to), we *can* contribute more confidently to meetings, speak up in our friendship groups or express our true feelings to our loved ones. We want to know that we'll have the courage to ask for a raise, join an art class or get out on the dance floor at a wedding. But beyond these motivating factors, I believe there's a far more significant need at stake.

On the surface, clients ask me to help them feel more confident or at least portray confidence, but when we scratch the surface, a larger truth emerges: what they're really searching for is an *inherent sense of self-worth, even with their imperfections*. Confidence is so much more than getting others to validate your worthiness; it's about cultivating a direct line to that worth for yourself, *believing* in that worth, and then living from a place where you feel a genuine sense of self-belief.

Having the courage to speak up: Clare's story

I saw a wonderful example of this once I started working with Clare. Her predominantly extroverted peers were quick off the mark with ideas, but their suggestions were not always well considered.

While spending six weeks in my group program, The Confidence Course, Clare set herself a challenge to speak up at least once in each of our weekly group calls. In this safe environment, she practised sharing ideas and I encouraged her to do so 'imperfectly'. By week four, Clare decided she would take on the same challenge in her workplace. Before her next team meeting, she reviewed the agenda and thought about where she most wanted to contribute. When the time came, she addressed the group quickly before anyone else had the chance to speak and when one of her co-workers went to interject, Clare pressed on regardless.

Owning and accepting her introversion had become important to Clare, so when she shared her idea, she was open about the fact that this was an initial thought only and she would like time to tease it out further. To her surprise, a couple of her colleagues and her manager supported her.

In that one meeting, Clare changed the way she views herself. She no longer defines herself as someone who doesn't have the confidence (or the right) to contribute her ideas and she has stopped believing she needs to be extroverted to have something of value to add. She now acknowledges that she's an intelligent woman with valuable content to offer.

When we behave authentically and start to build a deep and genuine sense of self-belief, we are well placed to reap the many benefits of having confidence.

These include:

- pursuing opportunities that make life fulfilling;
- believing that you are lovable;
- building genuine friendships;
- having boundaries;
- expressing yourself creatively;
- sharing your talents;
- networking;
- leading others;
- navigating work politics;
- being resilient;
- resolving conflict;
- public speaking, and
- feeling at peace with yourself.

Susan Cain says that 'knowing things isn't enough; you need to be able to present that knowledge, as well'. For introverts, it's this 'presenting' that often poses a problem. Like Shanti, you might be one of the smartest people in the room, but maybe you don't offer your ideas for fear of criticism. It's likely you sometimes see this hesitation in people close to you too. Maybe a friend who writes exquisite poetry but never puts her work out into the world, or another who wants to exhibit his photography but fears it's not good enough, or the person who is still studying because she needs just one more qualification before she's truly 'ready' to apply for a role. Externalising the internal doesn't come naturally to most introverts, and it's especially difficult when it requires that their knowledge be shared with large groups of people.

～

Research shows that a lack of confidence impacts women more often than men.

And low confidence has an even greater impact for women than not progressing at the same rate as male colleagues. In a series of tests, hundreds of university students (men and women) were given spatial problems to solve. Though many of the men didn't know how to solve the questions, they at least attempted to answer every question whereas women tended to skip questions if they weren't confident they could answer correctly. In the first test, men outperformed the women. However, after the women were told that they *had* to complete all the questions, they performed equally as well as the men.

How many opportunities do women miss out on over the course of their lives simply because they have so little faith in their abilities that they don't even try?

When confidence is so integral to even *attempting* success, it stands to reason that, for women in particular, introverted behaviours likely compound an already existing gender gap.

The social cost of this gender confidence gap is easily measured in the business world. Research shows that companies with more women in leadership roles perform significantly better and have better working conditions, not to mention better policies for families and more diversity in their teams. These companies also show more innovation, are more productive and have greater profits. Despite this, women around the world are paid 17 per cent less than men, and only 10 per cent of Fortune 500 companies globally are run by women. Many studies have shown that when women make money and lead companies, they do more good on a societal level than men in equivalent circumstances do.

It isn't just good for an individual woman or her immediate family when she succeeds, it's good for everyone, but without the confidence to throw her name in the hat, nobody benefits. If she also happens to be an introvert, this can put her at even more of a disadvantage.

Exploring and addressing this gender gap in confidence is vital; however, it's important to remember that many men struggle with confidence, too. I know this because I've worked with wonderful, intelligent, sensitive men buckling under the pressures of living up to the version of confidence being thrust upon them, and have seen that for them, this can be doubly challenging. They aren't just battling against society's idea of extroverted confidence; they are up against the very idea of what it is to be a man. After all, a 'real man' – a 'man's man' – is confident.

An online search of the terms 'men and confidence' returns thousands of results for papers and articles; however, most of these focus on the confidence gap between women and men. The default assumption seems to be that confidence is a given for men. Little boys are more likely to be pushed towards display-ing 'manly' or confident behaviours than girls are, regardless of whether those behaviours come naturally to them. As adults, men have fewer forums in which to express their vulnerabilities. If they stay true to their nature and refuse to role-play extroverted confidence, they are likely to find themselves being overtaken by their more extroverted peers. If they assume a confident façade in their work or public life, they may get further. But, eventually, the toll of being someone they're not catches up with them – often in the form of depression, anxiety, or perhaps, disconnection and apathy.

How can introverts close this confidence gap?

When an introvert expresses a desire to build their confidence, the available advice is often based on the premise that they will need to alter their behaviour (and personality) to meet the 'extrovert ideal'. Ambitious introverts may try to close the confidence gap by faking it 'til they make it and in some situations this can help as you work towards building genuine confidence, but for almost all introverts, presenting an extroverted face to the world has an enormous cost that is harder to measure than wages and job titles.

Over time, this kind of role-playing creates the type of stress that can erode your sense of self. Imagine that your true nature is a big, colourful beachball. Now, picture jumping into a swimming pool and holding that ball under the water as you try to swim laps. If your goal is to look natural while doing this or outpace the other swimmers, that's going to be pretty tough.

You might be able to keep that ball down for a few minutes, but eventually, the effort will exhaust you. And the harder you've forced the ball down, the higher it will fly when it bursts out of the water, as it inevitably will. Pretending is a huge struggle. None of us can be our best, most authentic selves when we're holding down this beachball, and we can't be our healthiest selves, either.

In *The Myth of Normal,* renowned Canadian physician and author Gabor Maté recounts how, when reviewing the research on chronic illnesses he'd been treating for more than 30 years, he came to the conclusion that being nice and people-pleasing at the expense of expressing true feelings does very real damage to our health. Maté identifies a pattern of behaviours that show up most often in people with chronic illnesses:

- ignoring one's own needs for the emotional needs of others;
- rigidly identifying with one's social role, duty and responsibility;
- being 'overdriven' due to being convinced that one needs to justify one's existence by doing and giving;
- repressing healthy, self-protective anger; and
- believing two things: that one is responsible for how others feel, and that one must never disappoint anyone.

The link between these traits and disease is often overlooked or missed completely, and Maté believes this is because this way of being is the norm in our culture. In fact, many of these behaviours are even seen as admirable strengths rather than the 'future liabilities' they are. We learn these behaviours as we grow up, and, eventually, they become automatic.

When these automatic behaviours override our body's natural warning signs – the vital emotions such as anger, fear or low mood – the problems really begin. Instead of attending to those warnings by confronting the source of our anger, comforting ourselves or taking time to restore our energy, we ignore our physical needs, which creates significant stress. Chronic stress of any kind places the nervous system in a heightened state, but Maté argues that suppressing emotions *consciously* is even more damaging.

We'll explore this connection between the emotional and the physical more in Part Three: Courage, and look at ways of countering these automatic behaviours, which is especially relevant information for introverts. Based on what I've observed of my own behaviour and that of my clients, my guess is that introverts exhibit these personality features far more frequently than extroverts. Generally speaking, introverts prefer a quieter, less dramatic existence, and they have a tendency to overthink, so it seems logical that we'd be more inclined than extroverts to avoid confrontation and to people-please.

It's a pattern common in women regardless of whether they're introverted – we often stay quiet to avoid rocking the boat. Talented women judge themselves more harshly than men and from a very young age girls are praised when they exhibit self-control, setting up the ongoing desire to be 'good'.

Since introverts also tend to be more self-aware and introspective, it's also possible that there are times when we're even *aware* of the feelings we are suppressing, making a conscious and detrimental choice to go against our body's warning signs.

When we're not being true or standing up for ourselves, the damage isn't limited to the individual self, either. If you have children in your life or you lead a team, consider what others learn about how to be in the world by watching you smile while doing something you hate. What will they think when they see you swallowing your feelings to placate someone else? What might they learn about how to manage their own feelings, resolve conflict and stand their ground when they observe you always deferring? The behaviour you model will affect the choices they'll make, which in turn, will impact their self-worth.

As we reflect on the discomfort of doing things differently, we need to ask ourselves some tough questions: is another person's comfort worth that much to us? Do we have the courage to face the difficult feelings that often accompany being true to ourselves?

Introverts often wrestle with the feeling that we probably need to change to fit in and make the most of our lives while instinctively knowing that if we want to be genuinely happy, we also need to be true to ourselves. This instinct tallies with another of Maté's theories: that we need to live authentically and respond to our emotions to be healthy. It's the uncertainty about how to operate effectively in an extroverted world that brings so many introverts to my door.

The struggle to balance a desire for confidence with a desire to be true to ourselves is one I know well myself and something I've been researching for decades. On the following pages, I'll share many of the concepts that have worked for my clients and me. Some may seem abstract, others you'll already be familiar with, and a few, you may have already tried. It's my hope that you'll feel inspired to choose one or two of these concepts to put into action immediately as you begin your journey to quiet confidence.

TWO

How I came to be interested in confidence

If I had to define my relationship with confidence, it would be 'complicated'. I've never been particularly drawn to the word 'confidence' and in fact, for most of my life, the word was a slight turn-off because of the image it conjured. I know a lot of my clients feel similar.

From the age I became aware of confidence, I viewed it as something other people aspired to. An introverted child in a family of extroverts, I preferred to stay safely in the background. I didn't fit into the world the same way my parents or sister did, and my 'oversensitive' nature was more a source of frustration than something to be celebrated.

It wasn't until I turned 30 and enrolled in a transcendental meditation (TM) course that I began cultivating the insight to really listen to and start to trust myself. It took time and practise, but eventually, something within me shifted. Author Glennon Doyle describes this internal wisdom as the 'Knowing' – the sense that you're finally in touch with the deepest truth within yourself. And that even if this truth isn't what the world has told you to be, listening is your only option.

I realised that I had long been subscribing to a mainstream dream. In trying to create the 'right' kind of life for our family, I was often conforming and people-pleasing. I wrestled with the idea that I should take a corporate job and give up the dream of starting my own business. I said yes to the parents' committee at school, even though group settings were my least favourite thing. My husband and I put ourselves under pressure to send our girls to private schools, despite it being outside our earning capacity. It was years before I came to recognise that every time I said yes to something that really wasn't right for us, I was moving myself and my family away from the things that most mattered.

What started as a glimmer of knowing continued to grow over the following decade as I took small steps towards being more true to myself. I continued practising meditation daily and worked with a psychologist, and both of these things led me to discover that I wanted to work with people who were struggling like I had been.

Finally, I had the courage to act on this insight when I enrolled in coaching training. I gave up my role as a business manager for film makers and found what felt like my true place in the world when I opened the doors of my practice. I let my intuition guide me and offered services that fused with my natural interests and life experience. At the urging of a mentor, I opened my own practice in the heart of Melbourne to service corporate clients. I began getting requests for keynotes and workshops, and I said yes to these, even though public speaking terrified me.

Outwardly, I was ticking a lot of 'success' boxes, and though I loved my life, I couldn't escape the feeling that I should be just a little more outgoing, stand up for myself more, be a bit more animated on stage, be a bit more . . . *confident*. I'd made so much progress, yet here I was, still butting up against the feeling that I still wasn't confident in the ways that mattered.

My client list was filled with thoughtful, intelligent people struggling with their own feelings of low confidence. I work with lawyers who found the law too competitive; creatives who found selling themselves difficult; bankers who wanted roles with more meaning; and not-for-profit workers who wanted more courage and confidence. Though extroverts are just as susceptible to experiencing crippling doubt in certain areas as introverts (you only have to look to Hollywood for examples of this), they weren't the people seeking me out. Overwhelmingly, my clients are introverts, and around 80 per cent of them are either INFJs or INFPs.

The acronyms INFJ and INFP represent just two of the sixteen personality types identified by Katherine Briggs and her daughter, Isabel Briggs Meyers. They took Jung's two fundamental attitude types – introverts and extroverts – and divided them into sixteen more detailed personality types. By asking a specific set of questions, they were able to determine an individual's four most dominant character traits, and sort them into one of these sixteen types.

The test they developed is still widely used around the world, and I encourage you to take it on the 16personalities website. It can be very enlightening.

I'm an INFJ, which means my four dominant traits are introverted (I), intuitive (N), feeling (F) and judging (J). INFJs and INFPs are the rarest personality types, so it was fascinating to me that in a city of over five million people, these people were so over-represented at my practice. *Why are so many INFJs and INFPs (and a few other variations of 'I' personality types) struggling so much with confidence?* I wondered. *And how do so many of them find me?* I can only assume that the description of my ideal client on my website calls them to me in some way. I describe my ideal client as someone who:

- wants to know themselves more deeply in order to quiet their self-doubt;
- sometimes feels like an imposter;
- has a vigilant 'inner critic' (and is maybe a little perfectionistic);
- describes themselves as an introvert, sensitive or someone who thinks deeply;
- hopes to make a positive difference in the world;
- values the idea of being creative, even if they don't have a traditionally creative pursuit;
- likes the idea of 'living consciously';
- cares about living in alignment with their values;
- wants to live a purposeful life;
- cares less about the external measures of 'success' and more about being true to themselves;
- feels restored by spending time in nature and cares about taking care of our planet;
- describes themselves as spiritual (even if they aren't entirely sure what that means to them).

If this sounds like you, it's no surprise that this book called your name. Month after month, for years, I fielded the same question: 'How can I build my self-belief?', and in 2020, with people reporting higher rates of anxiety following the global pandemic, I finally decided to follow my curiosity and throw myself into researching confidence. I started by looking for answers to three key questions:

1. What exactly is *real* confidence?
2. How does introversion impact confidence?
3. Which approaches are most effective when helping introverts build true confidence?

The more I read, the more questions I had. Why do some people seem to possess an innate sense of confidence, while others experience so much more self-doubt? Where do some individuals get the confidence to boldly chase their dreams, while others (usually of equal talent, ambition and ability) hesitate to enter the race at all? Why are some of us so hard on ourselves, while others seem able to brush off setbacks and bounce back from adversity so easily?

Perhaps the biggest question of all was how can introverts access the benefits of confidence without having to act like extroverts? Role-playing your way through life is no way to live, and as Gabor Maté pointed out, it's also a great risk to your physical and mental wellbeing. When you pretend to be something you are not, again and again, you send your soul a message: *You're not good enough as you are*, and whatever real confidence you have is at risk of being eroded.

To offer the introverts I work with better strategies, it became clear that I'd need to explore a different type of confidence entirely:

one more enduring than the one they'd been told to aspire to. It would need to be much more attainable for them and also play to their natural gifts and abilities. But first, I had to answer that first question: What exactly is confidence?

What exactly is confidence?

I knew what I thought confidence was, but to find out if my 21st-century definition was correct, I went back to the very beginning – to the etymology of the word and the birth of the very concept of 'self-confidence'.

The Latin roots of 'confidence' are *com* (usually meaning 'with' or 'together') and *fidere* (to trust). In the 1400s, around the time the word was first recorded, it described a trust or a belief in the veracity of another person. And just fifty years later, this definition had expanded to include trust in oneself: 'reliance on one's own powers, resources, circumstances or self-assurance'.

Reading these definitions was a light bulb moment for me. Framed in this way, confidence seems infinitely more attractive – and much more attainable. Guiding people to cultivate a deep 'trust' in themselves and their abilities, while helping them build the skills so they could work 'with' others as well as themselves is of genuine interest to me.

I was relieved to discover that there are *other* versions of confidence to choose from than the extroverted styles we introverts have been shown and then forced to mimic. After years of researching confidence and working with clients, it's now my belief that we don't have to play an extrovert's game to build true confidence and reach our goals. Loud confidence isn't for us – we're seeking a way of moving through the world that allows us to be humble, generous, thoughtful – and quietly confident.

Collective confidence

As I continued to look beyond the Western paradigm of confidence, I found versions that felt much more aligned with the word's true origins: 'with' and 'trust'. Brash, bold confidence isn't the only flavour on the global menu, and what's more, it doesn't play well in cultures with less individualistic outlooks than our own.

The cultures of Sweden, Denmark and Finland, for example, place more emphasis on egalitarianism and consensus-building than ours does. In these countries, a loud, aggressive or self-promoting style will be unlikely to win you many fans. There are bound to be people from these countries who do embrace a louder, pushier style of confidence, but it isn't the cultural norm.

The 'Confucian belt' of China, Japan, Korea and Vietnam, also displays an aversion to Western-style confidence. Though each is very different, the cultures of these countries are rooted in 'collectivism', which prioritises the benefit of the group over the importance of the individual. When group harmony is highly valued, humility, modesty and inner strength are celebrated. Standing out or self-promoting is often viewed as inappropriate or even arrogant. In these societies, it's a person's actions and accomplishments that validate their expertise or competence, not what they say about those things.

Each country has its own approach to confidence. In Japan, the word *hikari* (which translates to 'light' or 'radiance') is sometimes associated with a quiet, understated type of confidence that isn't boastful or showy. The Chinese word *wu wei* describes a similar style of confidence rooted in inner peace and a sense of security. A leader who embraces *wu wei* is likely to rely on their own wisdom in the face of uncertainty, and see the value in trusting their intuition rather than relying on external predictions or expectations.

In South Korea, the twin phenomena of *jeong* and *woori* feed into each other to create a unique culture. *Jeong* is described as a feeling of filial affection, closeness and interconnectedness that develops over time and through shared experiences. Even if these experiences are negative, a person can still feel *jeong* for a difficult colleague or family member. *Woori* is a feeling of belonging so deep that it's more of a dissolving of the self into the group than a feeling of belonging to a group. In the context of *woori*, an individual's problem at work becomes the whole department's problem. At home, it's not 'my house' but 'our house'. *Woori* occurs at all levels of society and transcends hierarchical structures, allowing problems to be solved collectively – bosses and employees will tackle challenges together as equals, and often find more creative solutions because of this culture of *woori*.

In the 1980s, American researchers coined a term to define an 'Eastern' style of confidence that places more value on inner strength and composure than on bravado or assertiveness: what they described as a 'quiet confidence'. I was delighted when I discovered this research because intuitively, these are the ideas I had been tuning into for many years. I knew that confidence needed to be egalitarian, and that an inner sense of harmony and humility were essential. But maybe most important of all, these findings pointed to the fact that connecting with our own inner wisdom (what the Japanese call our 'light'), rather than looking outside or measuring ourselves against others, was where we could find an enduring and meaningful version of confidence that would remain with us for life.

~

Closer to home, I found examples of quiet confidence in the Indigenous cultures of Australia and New Zealand, as well as in aspects of the Indigenous cultures of America, Canada and Brazil. While each group is unique, with its own culture, language and traditions, most are rooted in a collectivist approach to life and problem-solving, where the good of the community and nature are prioritised over the needs of individuals. The strong sense of connection (not ownership) that First Peoples feel towards the land and the ancestral spirits of their people contributes to a deep connection that fosters confidence.

Spirituality also plays an important role in both Indigenous communities and building quiet confidence. Whether we find our spirituality in nature, through ceremonial rituals, meditation or prayer, it reinforces our ability to connect with and draw strength from something bigger than ourselves, and this can be incredibly important. It anchors us in the wider world and reminds us that we are part of something much, much bigger – tiny cogs in a huge and awesome machine.

Similarly, external connections and sources of strength can build our personal confidence, but so can connecting with a deeper sense of authenticity, or what we might call our own *inner light*. Having a genuine connection to who you are gives you access to that which gives your life meaning, building your resilience in the face of change, adversity or fear. In Indigenous communities, these experiences are often expressed through art and stories, which immortalises their importance and adds to a sense of confidence, connection and resilience not only for the individual, but also for the culture they are part of.

Individualism versus collectivism: The push and pull of fitting in

Western culture's reverence for individualism is problematic for many reasons, not least because it flies in the face of our desire to belong, which creates a tension within us at our very core: we are animals wired to want to belong. Society encourages us to do this when it pressures us to conform at school, work and in sports, and 'fit in' with our friend groups. The notion that 'we're all in this together' is drilled into us from an early age; however, it's not the only message we're receiving. At the same time, we are encouraged to be an individual in the 'right' ways, so we aren't seen as belonging *too much*. After all, nobody respects the 'sheep' or 'lemmings' who mindlessly follow the crowd.

As a result, many of us walk a tightrope between wanting to belong and striving to be an individual – balancing our desire to be part of the crowd with the pressure to excel in our chosen fields and do better than our peers. (No wonder we're confused!) The mixed messages we're being sent are likely rooted in our more 'collectivist' history.

Before the industrial revolution, many communities were small and isolated, and life was challenging. What mattered most was the substance of a person, whether they were a moral, trust-worthy and hard-working member of the community. More value was placed on working towards the benefit of the group than the success of the individual.

The industrial revolution had a dramatic effect on this culture of character. As people left small, rural communities to find opportunities in growing cities, the paradigm of the 'ideal self' began shifting from the serious, disciplined, honourable self to a self that could be quickly assessed, admired and assigned value by strangers.

When a person arrived in a new town or city, how they were *perceived* mattered more than ever before. They relied on strangers to give them their next job, accommodation, friendship or help them gain influence. Presenting themselves in a way that meant strangers would see them as trustworthy, competent and likeable became an essential survival skill, and outgoing extroverts were better positioned to take advantage of this than introverts. These changes sowed the seed for a 'culture of personality' that still exists today.

In its infancy, the culture of personality played out in the society pages of newspapers as individuals got rich and became well known. In the 1920s, movie stars took over and the collective fascination with individuals continued to evolve, eventually becoming what we have today: a democratic free-for-all where anyone with a smartphone and social media account can offer themselves to the world as a 'personality' to be followed, admired and celebrated.

THREE

Quiet confidence

My definition of 'quiet confidence' has little in common with celebrity culture. It's more aligned with the ancient wisdom described by different cultural groups. It doesn't emphasise being famous or loud or always knowing the answer or being the most powerful decision-maker in a room. Instead, it places value on feeling centred, grounded and connected to your own inner 'light'. It values connection, collaboration and contribution, and is about embodying a genuine sense of self-worth, self-respect, self-acceptance and self-compassion. For me, quiet confidence is rooted in three things:

1. **Trust** that deep within each of us, there's a part of ourselves that is already confident, and with the right kind of support, we can find our way back to this time and again. Trust that we know our own values and strengths. Trust that we can choose our direction and be resilient when things

don't go to plan. Trust that we are worthy and enough, right now, just as we are. This kind of confidence doesn't rely on external validation – it's not about comparing, competing, achieving or striving but rather, knowing and being yourself. It's the kind of confidence that grows as we grow. My client Deb describes it as the kind of confidence she experiences as 'a felt sense' in the body. She knows it when she teaches a yoga class by following her intuition but loses it entirely when she gets caught up in the negative voices in her head.

2. **Connection** not only with our true self, but also to the trust we have in that self. Connection to people, places and experiences that feed our true self as well as connection to something bigger than ourselves. For me, it was all of these things that gave me the courage to pursue my most closely held dreams.

3. **Worth**. Not in the measurable sense of wealth, beauty, titles or possessions, but in the sense of an emotional awareness that we are enough exactly as we are because every single individual has inherent value and is worthy of love and belonging. Clare's willingness to let go of the need to be perfect is an excellent example. She came to see that her true worth was most easily expressed by engaging her innate strengths, not pretending to be something she is not.

Worth is something clinician Kent Hoffman feels strongly about. During a class at graduate school, a professor of Kent's said something that immediately changed the way he saw other people.

He said, **'Every person you will ever meet has infinite worth.'**
In Kent's work as a developmental researcher in psychology, he's
spent time with prisoners, cancer patients and homeless people
on Skid Row. After years of working 'in places where there is
suffering', he has come to believe that struggling with self-worth
is a universally human condition.

While working with at-risk homeless teens, Kent asked them
to write down a sentence or two about whatever the voice in their
head was most frequently saying. In light of the tough experiences and difficult circumstances they were facing, the negative
thoughts they shared made sense. But when he asked students in
his university teaching seminars to do the same exercise, he found
that they wrote virtually the same phrases, despite being 'low-
risk' twenty-somethings in the privileged position of attending
university:

- *I'm not enough.*
- *I'm not sure I matter.*
- *I'm not attractive enough/smart enough/effective enough/
  good enough.*
- *No matter how hard I try, something inside me isn't lovable.*
- *Even if I make an effort, I'll likely fail in some way.*

Self-worth is something I wrestled with myself throughout
my life. My family moved around a lot when I was young and
starting a new school every year or so meant I had no sense of
belonging to a friendship group or a place. I spent a lot of time
adapting to fit in. Because my parents and sister were extroverts
who thrived on meeting new people and immersing themselves in
group settings, I sensed that there was something wrong with me

when I felt vulnerable or needed time alone. I carried the same negative thoughts as the teenagers and students Kent Hoffman worked with.

It wasn't until I began hearing similar stories from clients that I came to understand that I wasn't alone. The most healing experience in my own life has been discovering that we're all just as human as each other. Every one of us is vulnerable, we all have worries and flaws and at the same time, we also have unique gifts and strengths. It became apparent to me after working with thousands of truly wonderful clients that *each of us really does have infinite worth*. I could see something special in everyone who came into my room which made it easy to lean into the belief that each of us is – as Kent says – 'an unrepeatable jewel'. Knowing and believing this is the single most important step we can take towards tapping in to true confidence.

Though Kent had grown up putting people into categories, and assigning them worth based on societal measures, after hearing those words from his professor, he understood that we all share the same miraculous infinite worth. Today, he spreads the message that no person is worth more than any other person.

The idea that all of us are equally valuable is one many of us have heard, but based on my own experience and Kent's examples, it's a message most of us don't believe – especially when it comes to ourselves.

Self-esteem

Self-esteem is closely linked to self-worth and also to confidence, but it's worth pausing to unpack the differences between these terms because they inform and influence each other. Interestingly, though people with high self-esteem generally find it easier to act with more confidence, the reverse isn't always the case. Self-confidence is *not* always accompanied by high self-esteem. People can be full of confidence but not necessarily 'esteem' themselves.

Hiding behind bravado: Caroline's story

Many years ago, when my business was based in the city, I spent several years working with executives. Caroline, a financial consultant in her mid-thirties, was one of these clients. We met when the firm she worked for invited a number of coaches to interview for the opportunity to support some of their high-potential leaders. After participating in these interviews, I was surprised to find out that Caroline had chosen me as her coach. She presented as confident, assertive and abrupt, and her manner was aloof and almost unfriendly – not the type of personality who usually sought me out. I questioned if she really even needed me.

I was still in the early days of my coaching career and felt somewhat intimidated by her abrasive manner. In our first session, when I asked her what she hoped to achieve through working with me, she answered, 'Just what's on the brief from the firm. I want to shore up my leadership skills and fast-track a promotion.' We went through an assessment of what Caroline believed the required leadership qualities for her next role were and evaluated where she felt she needed my help.

We decided to start our work together by focusing on measurable skills like hitting budget targets and meeting other key performance indicators. In reality, Caroline was skilled at putting together deals and known for being a tough negotiator, and she was already doing well in her target areas, so I wasn't sure that I was going to make much of a difference. At our third meeting, I decided to be vulnerable myself. I opened up about my concerns about how much I'd be able to help her. Caroline softened a little that day, and when we met the following week, her manner was markedly different.

For the first time, she spoke candidly and confessed that her work persona was largely an act masking a significant sense of imposter syndrome. Underneath her abrasive exterior, she was actually a sensitive introvert. As a child, she'd been compared unfavourably with her outgoing and popular older brother and had felt largely unsupported by her parents. At school, she had been misunderstood by classmates and frequently bullied in the playground. The school library had been her sanctuary at lunchtimes while weekends were mostly spent alone in her bedroom.

Thankfully, Caroline had been resilient enough to channel her energy into a love of learning. She set a goal of achieving academic success and went on to excel in her studies. But the pain of those younger years lingered, and she developed protective ways of interacting with the world. When required to speak in front of her peers at university, she did what many introverts do to mask their fear: she adopted extroverted qualities as well as a steely exterior. This was the same mask she now wore in her workplace, and it was this version of Caroline that I saw at our first meeting. It was only after building a trusting relationship that I came to know that Caroline's abrasive exterior hid a lot of sadness and self-doubt.

Like many people who lack a genuine sense of self-esteem, Caroline hid her true personality from everyone. While she felt confident in the skillsets she had developed, she had very little belief in her true self. She lacked an inherent sense of worthiness and, at her core, believed that she wasn't even lovable. When it came to building meaningful relationships, she felt that her only option was to hide her true personality, but this kept her isolated from friends and workmates.

Like Caroline's colleagues and managers, I failed to notice the subtle signs of vulnerability she had been sending. As is common with women who struggle with imposter syndrome, Caroline was putting herself under enormous pressure to succeed, working longer hours than her colleagues and investing no energy in her social life. She was almost always in a state of stress. After long days at work, she told me she often lay awake catastrophising – worrying her boss would 'find her out' and fire her without the reference required to get a new job.

Over the ensuing months, I helped Caroline understand herself better and together we began to question the stories she had been telling herself. We examined the parts of her personality she had long been afraid to embrace. As we worked to help Caroline connect with her authentic self, I invited her to access the courage inside her by changing her actions in small, subtle ways.

This meant dialling down the over-achiever part of her personality and allowing herself to be more open, generous and vulnerable. When a colleague asked her if she was okay after a particularly tough day, Caroline took a chance and let her guard down for the first time. After confessing that she felt exhausted and overwhelmed, the two of them spent several minutes talking. The next day, that same colleague offered to take one of her tasks off her plate. After this positive experience, Caroline began practising being more open with others. Weeks later, she joined her colleagues for after-work drinks on a Friday, and – to her surprise – she enjoyed being with them in a more relaxed setting.

Generally speaking, confidence relates to how we feel about our own ability to do something, while self-worth relates to the belief that we are *always* worthy and of equal value to everyone else. Ideally, both of these things are measured internally, and, when belief in them is strong, they are unlikely to be shaken by external influences.

In contrast, self-esteem relates to how we 'esteem' ourselves – i.e., how we think of ourselves and estimate our worth, often in the eyes of others and generally, at a given point in time. How we gauge this can depend on how we stack up against markers of success (e.g., career status, physical appearance, material wealth, friends, academic or sporting achievements), and how we imagine other people perceive us. When we believe we are worthy and others view us positively, we experience the positive feelings of high self-esteem. When we believe we are less worthy than others, we experience the negative feelings of low self-esteem.

When defined this way, self-esteem is volatile and changeable. We might only think that we are valuable and worthy in moments when we're behaving at our best; when our relationships are harmonious; when we're working in certain roles; when we are achieving our goals or 'maximising our potential'. And if we're tired, unwell or if our mood happens to be low, this evaluation of ourselves is likely to be distorted and inaccurate.

A more helpful view of self-esteem comes closer to the concept of intrinsic worth. High self-esteem involves being generally accepting of yourself, respecting and appreciating yourself and having '*intrinsic value and worth despite your human weaknesses*'. It means feeling that you're worthy of taking up space in the world and able to enjoy what life has to offer – even during times when you're imperfect.

The good news is that it's universally agreed upon that we can grow both our confidence *and* our self-esteem at any stage in life and while this book is ultimately about building quiet confidence, it is also designed to change the relationship you have with yourself, which will provide a genuine boost to your self-esteem and an enduring sense of self-worth.

Are we born with confidence?

As I began to unpack the concept of quiet confidence, I came to realise that I've seen it in action when I occasionally encounter people who appear to have *been born* with a quiet kind of confidence. These people have a presence that you feel as soon as you meet them. They're in tune with themselves, don't shy away from making hard decisions, they're willing to speak up about what they believe in, comfortable to set appropriate boundaries and they know how to ask for what they want.

They know their own minds and express their feelings openly and easily. They're aware of their needs and comfortable sharing them, which makes them easy people to have relationships with. Their open communication means you're rarely left guessing how they feel and even when they disagree with you, their words are never loaded or unkind. They air their feelings as they arise, and their directness is gentle and not intended to wound. I marvel at their ability to stand their ground with humility and the positive way people respond when they do this. There's no unnecessary drama, no heightened emotion, just an acceptance that they have an opposing view.

These same people also appear to tap in to their innate 'knowing' and have the ability to sit in the truth of who they are (weaknesses included). They choose their own paths without comparing themselves to others. They are open and curious, but they trust their own judgement and for the most part, they're sure of their opinions. They're decisive, considerate, courageous and calm while at the same time, willing to be vulnerable. People love and respect them for all of these qualities.

Even though this style of confidence is humble and generous, there are times when people find it disarming, and I've discovered that a few still want to shut them down. In a world that tells us to be confident *but not too confident*, it's inevitable that even people who have this innate confidence still sometimes question their self-belief. This is possibly what makes them so likeable.

Perhaps you're thinking, *That's great for someone who is born with this kind of confidence, but what about the rest of us?* Behavioural geneticist Robert Plomin, who conducted the longest and largest study linking genes with confidence, believes that the correlation between genes and confidence might be as high as 50 per cent. Other experts point to the more accepted theory that the 'Big Five' personality traits (openness, conscientiousness, extroversion, agreeableness and neuroticism) are about 50 per cent genetic, while attributes such as optimism and confidence are around 25 per cent inherited.

Whatever the exact figure, it's clear that genes do play a significant role where confidence is concerned. Hundreds of studies scrutinising DNA have led scientists to believe that quite a lot of our personality is set from conception. It seems our genes influence everything from how shy or motivated we are, to how likely we might be to engage in criminal behaviour.

Even if we weren't born with an innate sense of confidence, this doesn't mean that we're destined to live less authentic lives. As powerful as nature is, scientists now believe that nurture is powerful enough to alter nature's original programming by turning genes on and off. This doesn't just apply to how we are nurtured in childhood, either. Habitual thinking has the power to create physical change and new neural pathways in our brain, and this can not only override genetics but also change our brain chemistry through something called neural plasticity, which is the ability of neural networks in our brain to change through growth and reorganisation. Like so much of our behaviour, confidence is a malleable attribute that can increase or decrease depending on the actions we take. It's something we can grow, at any stage of life.

Most of the people I work with role-model *the potential we all have* within us to grow and develop when we make a choice to capitalise on this neural plasticity. While a lucky few are born with an innate sense of self-belief, most of us have to work at confidence building.

After seeing some of the profound changes clients have made in their lives, I have come to believe that *anyone can train themselves to be confident.* Through diligent practice, we can learn to trust our inner wisdom, to make choices that are right for us, and we can find the courage to pursue any of our dreams. We can break our people-pleasing patterns and act and speak from a place of deep self-awareness and worth. We can value ourselves in the same way that those innately confident people do while recognising that feeling deeply confident has nothing to do with being perfect.

Whether you were born with a sensitive nature, struggled to learn in school, had a parent who told you that you weren't good enough, were bullied as a teen or rejected by a partner, the result is often the same: you emerge from those experiences feeling unworthy in some way. Consequently, you don't feel you can advocate for yourself easily, but you pretend to be fine. You say, 'Oh, that's okay,' when really it isn't. Resentment often builds, frustration and anger are suppressed and, often, a tipping point is reached when those suppressed feelings manifest in other ways, e.g., a midlife crisis or even anxiety, depression or illness.

It doesn't have to be this way. Like so many of the people I work with, you can choose to cultivate confidence in a way that aligns with your personality and natural abilities. You can learn to speak from the most authentic part of yourself and embrace your innate worth. Best of all, you don't have to pretend to be someone else or stuff down your feelings in the process. In fact, the opposite is true. The truer to yourself you can be, the stronger your sense of confidence will become.

FOUR

My roadmap for building confidence

Embodying quiet confidence isn't about playing a role, but rather strengthening the confidence that already lives inside you. Depending on where you are in your journey with confidence, you may not believe this innate force exists, but in Part Two: Connection, I'll help you locate it. You'll know it because it's connected to your many strengths and aligned with things that truly matter to you.

As we progress, I'll encourage you to call on this force regularly and to proactively bring it to the fore in all areas of life. It may not be fully developed right now, but by flexing this muscle regularly, it will be. Through practice, it will come to be part of the essence of you and there's nothing more authentic than that.

You're likely to discover that the benefits of connecting with your confident self extend beyond the professional and social. It can give you access to more lightness and joy and become an anchor during turbulent times, which are things we all need in today's world.

The dream destination is the 'glorious middle'

It's impossible to ignore the many ways our world is becoming increasingly polarised, both literally and figuratively: as the chasm between rich and poor grows wider, political ideologies move away from each other and further from the centre. A few minutes spent scrolling through the comments section of any social media post (not something I do myself or recommend) can reveal the polarity that thrives around our dinner tables and in meeting rooms, schools and governments. The stress of picking a side and then defending those ideological views divides families, friends, colleagues and even countries.

Given the highly charged climate we now live in, it's not surprising that much of my working life is spent helping clients come back to the centre so they can live, work and love from a place I call the 'glorious middle'. Stability in a chaotic world starts on the inside. When we can tap in to a state of equanimity and calm in a world that is anything but, it helps us to access our innate sense of confidence.

Dr Daniel Siegel uses the word 'integration' to describe this middle ground. In his model of a healthy mind, all the components function well and are interconnected. When our mind isn't integrated, we can easily tip into an unhealthy state because we have strayed too far from the middle. He describes this using the analogy of floating down a river in a canoe. One bank of the river represents chaos and the other represents rigidity, which can only be maintained when we are controlling everything and everyone around us. If we drift too far towards chaos, we are filled with anxiety, instability and fear. Drift in the other direction, and we are inflexible, stuck and stagnate. (I imagine we might also experience conflict as we try to control people and situations.)

Our goal is to move to the middle of the river where the free-flowing water makes moving forward purposeful and easy. This part of the river represents a state that is calm, curious and connected. Any decisions we make from this place are likely to be guided by our sense of purpose and our values rather than desperation or fear.

To stay in this middle lane, I advocate using mindfulness practices that bring awareness to the body and our intuition – practices that connect us with our inner wisdom. The more skilled we become at tuning in to this wisdom and operating from this place of integration, the more freedom we have to live a grounded, centred life and move towards goals that truly matter to us. Living in this way breeds authenticity, self-worth and trust in the self – the ingredients of true confidence, rather than the kind of confidence that is currently glamorised by society.

When you begin this work, you may have an image in your head of the person you'd like to be by the end of it, and that's normal. Most of us do this because we buy into the message that the goal is to arrive at a place where we've 'worked it all out' and 'fixed' all the things. This is largely unhelpful because the destination is an illusion, and no book or course can get you there.

Instead, the real mission is to *make peace with who you are and where you are right now*, while still moving in the direction of your dreams. This means accepting that you will continue to make messy choices, say the wrong things sometimes and occasionally hurt people's feelings, because these are all part of human condition. Your humanness is not a burden, it's a miracle you can experience minute by minute once you learn to tap in to this truth.

Imagine that instead of focusing disproportionately on our weaknesses and trying to 'fix' the aspects of ourselves we perceive as falling short, we embrace them and ourselves in our totality and live from that wise and knowing space. How much energy might we have to devote to other things? How much more might we be able to contribute?

The four steps of my confidence journey

I've written this book to help you tap in to your innate strengths and the gifts that already live inside you so you can solidify the trust you have in yourself. It's my hope that in doing this, you might also find that you can accept yourself exactly as you are today and move – with a greater sense of quiet confidence – towards your goals, whatever they might be. Returning you to that middle ground might mean you can live a more centred and grounded life where you are fully and authentically yourself – with all of your wonderful imperfections.

Through research, interviews with experts and work with my clients and groups, I have developed a 'journey to confidence', which I've honed further in this book and distilled into four essential steps, each comprising part of the book.

Part One: Meaning

We'll start by taking a bird's-eye view of your life so you can become curious about the parts of your life that provide meaning. Meaning is maybe the most powerful fuel and the most valuable resource to give you the motivation to keep moving towards your goals. By tapping in to what is meaningful to you, you'll find it easier to recalibrate in small increments to ensure that you are living in alignment with your values every day.

Part Two: Connection

Next, you'll become better acquainted with the many aspects of your personality. We'll explore how each of these different 'selves' influences your behaviour and how you can engage with yourself with more kindness and compassion. We'll get curious about your natural strengths because these pave the pathway to true confidence, and we'll explore the importance of connection with other people.

Part Three: Courage

In this part of the book, you'll discover the benefits of stepping out of your mind and into your body or perhaps, more specifically, into your heart. Building confidence is a habit and, like all habits, it requires us to take action, even when we don't feel like it. I will invite you to stretch yourself in order to express confidence in a way that's meaningful and authentic for you.

Part Four: Presence

The final step is about cultivating and nurturing a centred and unshakeable style of confidence that is uniquely yours. We'll explore practices for offering yourself acceptance, compassion and grace so you can strengthen the presence you bring with you into every aspect of life. Presence isn't a destination, but rather the direction you will head towards for the rest of your life as you radiate confidence from the inside out.

How will we travel on this journey?

Now that you've seen the roadmap, you might be curious about how we'll be approaching each of the elements. The answer is slowly and with very small steps. This perhaps isn't what you were hoping to hear, and I understand that. We live in a time when decades of ageing can be unwound with an afternoon facelift; bodies can be sculpted by an eight-week exercise program and people barely out of their teens can become millionaires by betting on virtual currency. Our culture is attracted to dramatic transformations, and when we want to see change in an area of our life, we usually want the change to happen immediately.

As enticing as we find the idea of radical change, implementing it goes against our nature. We feel safest when things are familiar, so when there's an abnormality – whether it's a change in food, exercise, a routine or a behaviour – it often triggers a fear response in our brains, and consequently, we lose the power to think clearly and creatively.

Small changes, on the other hand, sidestep this response, making them a much more manageable and sustainable path to lasting change. This is probably why thinkers and philosophers over thousands of years across many cultures have advocated for this 'baby steps' approach. As Lao Tzu said, 'A journey of 100. miles starts with a single step.' In the bestselling book

Atomic Habits, James Clear uses scientific research and real-life examples to demonstrate the power of small, incremental changes to yield big results over time.

Kaizen, an organisational business philosophy used since the 1940s to transform entire industries, shares a lot of DNA with Clear's *Atomic Habits* – so much so that it's being increasingly embraced as an effective way to manage change at a more personal level. Progress compounds, and even the tiniest steps can lead to huge gains when taken consistently.

Applying kaizen to building confidence

It might seem unorthodox to be talking about a philosophy from the business and manufacturing world in a book about building personal confidence and self-worth, but I think you'll find many ways to put it to use in your own life. Fundamentally, kaizen is about making very small changes continuously to achieve a desired outcome.

As well as small steps, kaizen's principles include letting go of assumptions, being proactive and creative about problem solving, not even striving for perfection and holding on to the assumption that we can always be improving.

What makes small changes so effective?

When it comes to personal change, small steps can create new neural pathways in your brain, much like habitual thinking can. Any action, when repeated regularly, is a step towards creating a new habit, but as we touched on earlier, when this step is very small, it doesn't trigger the fear response the same way a radically different step does.

There is beauty in small, consistent changes, and best of all, introverts are wired for this type of change – it plays to our natural strengths. Woven through the chapters that follow, you'll find suggestions and exercises used in kaizen to help you move forward without fear. These simple practices can be performed (for free) again and again. Bit by bit, you'll build trust in yourself, become aware of your worth, gradually drifting closer to the centre of the river and the wonderful state of equanimity.

Rediscovering herself through a song: Helen's story

Around a decade ago in one of my day-long meditation workshops, a lovely lady in her seventies, who I'll call Helen, shared a story of embracing small change that I've never forgotten. It was late in the day, and I had been introducing participants to various different styles of meditation so that they could choose the one that best suited them. We'd been talking about creativity as a way of being mindful and in one brief exercise, we engaged in a group singing practice. It took a while for people to join in (as it turned out, few of us were confident singers), but people always found the experience uplifting. Afterwards, Helen sat quietly, looking vulnerable and I asked her how she found it. Her voice started to break as she spoke, but she was brave enough to tell her story. 'That is the first time since I was nine years old that I have sung a single note,' she said. Her eyes filled with tears as she went on to share that until that point, singing had been her most loved activity. She used to sing her heart out in the school choir until minutes before the final year concert when her insensitive teacher sidled up to her and said, 'You just mouth the words, Helen. You always sing out of key.' Mortified, Helen vowed to never sing again.

Almost everyone in the room was moved by her story. We all had our own tales of not feeling good enough at various moments in life, but Helen's experience was particularly sad. Imagining that little girl on stage having to perform while carrying such grief moved many of the women to tears. Knowing that for over sixty years Helen had not allowed herself the gift of song, seemed such a waste. Yet at the workshop that day, in a single moment, everything changed for Helen.

'As soon as the music started, I felt a wave of calm come over me and I decided I would let myself sing just this one song even if I was off-key,' she told us. 'And I can't tell you how incredible that felt. Now, I have sixty years of catching up to do. I'll begin with a single song every day and even if it means singing out of tune for the rest of my life, I'm going to do it anyway.'

A few months later, Helen sent me an email to let me know she had recently joined a community choir and the highlight of her week (and her life now) was coming together to sing.

Bring in mindfulness and self-compassion

A lot of the work you'll be doing on this confidence journey will involve reflection and enquiry, which aren't always easy tasks – especially if you happen to be starting from a place of not feeling so great about yourself. I advocate treading lightly when observing your thoughts and examining any revelations and I encourage you to do all of this work with an attitude of self-kindness. And even if you're not someone who is interested in meditation, the basic principles of mindfulness can help you to feel grounded and calm as you tackle change.

If you're new to mindfulness, think of it as just another word for awareness. When you bring your attention to any given moment, you begin to experience life as you're living it. For most of us, this isn't a regular habit. Often, our minds are ruminating on the past or worrying about the future, moving us away from the possibility of peace. Even when we do spend time in the present moment, we tend to make judgements of ourselves, of others and about life in general. The result is wanting the given moment to be different from what it is.

Being fully present means not only bringing your awareness back to the here and now, but appreciating the experience of this moment and accepting it for what it is. This involves creating a shift in the way that we interact with difficult thoughts and feelings, something we'll explore more in the following chapter, and it's also an opportunity to practise more self-compassion.

Compassion is best described as being sensitive to the experience of suffering (in others) coupled with a deep desire to alleviate that suffering. It involves an understanding that our shared human condition is fragile and vulnerable and requires a willingness to extend understanding to others when they fail or make mistakes. Interestingly, although our culture places a lot of emphasis on being kind to *others* when they are struggling, it isn't as vocal when it comes to directing this kindness inwards, even though doing this is incredibly important. When we show ourselves compassion, we reassure ourselves that we are valuable simply because we are human. The beautiful thing about knowing we have value – exactly as we are – is that it makes it easier for us to recognise the inherent value in other people, and vice versa.

Though many believe that building high self-esteem is the route to self-worth, others believe self-compassion is a more effective pathway to worth. As we focused on earlier, how we 'esteem' ourselves is very often dependent on how we measure up to other people or society's measures of success. If we don't feel special or superior in some way, our self-esteem suffers. By this definition, high self-esteem can only be maintained through a constant need to do more or feel better than others, and this degree of competition leads to a feeling of isolation and separation, which is the opposite of what we are wired for.

Self-compassion, on the other hand, emphasises connection – especially with ourselves. When we confront our own pain, recognise it as part of our human experience and show ourselves kindness rather than ignoring it or being self-critical, we care for ourselves in a profound way. Comparison doesn't factor into self-compassion, and for this reason, it offers far more emotional stability than self-esteem. Whether we have it isn't contingent on our successes or failures. Instead, it's an unlimited resource we can tap in to at any moment. Being able to rely on ourselves to acknowledge and embrace the truth of who we are gives us a direct line to our intrinsic worth, and alongside that, true confidence.

Although research indicates that self-compassion can be another one of those pre-existing personality traits, the good news is that it can be strengthened and developed through practice – especially mindfulness practices.

The steps that follow will help you to create a deeper connection with the truest version of yourself, while at the same time allowing you to see that all of the confidence you need is already within you.

Self-compassion exercise

Research psychologist and self-compassion pioneer Kristin Neff outlines the following three areas as the key elements of self-compassion:

1. Self-kindness vs self-criticism

Self-compassion involves sending warmth and kindness to ourselves when we make a mistake or we're dealing with difficult emotions. Instead of criticising ourselves or pretending we're not facing difficulty, we treat ourselves gently and kindly.

2. Shared experience vs isolation

When we remind ourselves that we're not alone in our suffering, we become less judgemental of our errors and more forgiving of ourselves, which in turn, makes us more accepting when others make mistakes. Remembering the shared experience helps us to feel less alone. Rather than focusing on differences, you begin to recognise how much you have in common with other people.

3. Mindfulness vs over-identification

Being mindful means taking a balanced view of your experience – not suppressing your emotions or exaggerating them in any way. This means you're less inclined to be swept up in overactive thinking and able to simply acknowledge your weaknesses, mistakes and negative emotions, while accepting yourself in a loving, non-judgemental way.

Try one or more of the exercises Kristin Neff and her colleagues recommend to build self-compassion:
- Catch yourself when you're experiencing a difficult emotion or speaking to yourself in a harsh way. Instead of engaging in your

usual patterns of negative thinking, try saying to yourself: *'This is difficult for me',* or *'I'm being incredibly hard on myself'.*

- Think about what you would say to a friend who was going through a similar experience. Write down a few phrases that you would say to them and repeat these to yourself.
- Place one or both hands over your heart in a difficult moment and take a couple of deep breaths. Pay attention to the soothing feeling of touch as you take a few breaths and repeat the self-compassion phrases you identified above. Research suggests that physical touch helps to release oxytocin into your body, creating a calming effect on your nervous system.
- Listen to a guided loving-kindness meditation, an ancient Buddhist practice designed to cultivate a benevolent attitude to yourself and others. Silently repeat three loving kindness phrases, directed at others and yourself, each night before going to bed.
- At the end of each day, write down three things you appreciate about yourself or three things you did well in your day.
- Write a self-compassionate letter to yourself, addressing yourself as though from the perspective of a kind and supportive friend. Read through your letter a couple of times during your week.

Introduction summary

- The version of confidence we've come to recognise in Western culture is what author Susan Cain calls the 'extrovert ideal'. *Quietly Confident* is an invitation to explore a different kind of confidence.
- People with low competence often over-estimate their abilities while those with high competence do the opposite.

- Different global cultures view confidence in different ways. Individualism isn't the only 'flavour' of confidence.
- Quiet confidence is about building trust in yourself, connecting with your values and strengths, and recognising that every individual (including you) has inherent value, regardless of where you are in your life.
- A healthy view of self-esteem is not about measuring yourself against others but rather, accepting, respecting and appreciating yourself right now.
- The four steps to confidence are finding meaning, creating connection with yourself and others, building courage and finding presence.
- The principles of kaizen, mindfulness and self-compassion will help you on your journey to building confidence.

Part One

Meaning

In the early days of my business, I vowed I would never do *any* public speaking. I had no plans to step on a stage and I wasn't even interested to run a small workshop. Any form of presenting to a group was out of the question for me. Despite this, I received many requests to share meditation tips (I'd been practising meditation for almost a decade) and gradually, I began considering running a very small meditation class for beginners.

Before I could find the courage to do this, I needed to understand *why* I would even consider tackling this fear. When I shared the idea with my daughters, they couldn't understand why I would put myself under this type of pressure. 'It's *your* business,' they said. 'You can do whatever you want!' (A compelling thought for teenage girls.) I knew this was true, and yet, at the same time, I had a strange sense that there was a deeper reason for me to take on this challenge. It somehow felt that public speaking was a calling to me.

Many introverts who find themselves in the public eye feel the same way. Across history, change makers such as Rosa Parks, Eleanor Roosevelt, Gandhi and Greta Thunberg described themselves as softly spoken or shy, and none desired the spotlight, each ended up on their path because they felt they had no choice. They felt compelled to share something with the world that was meaningful to them. They believed that what they were doing was truly right. Their actions were purposeful and meaningful, aligned with their values and, importantly, they knew they were making a difference in other people's lives.

When meaning is missing from our lives, or we drift away from things that matter to us, we feel it in our bodies. This might start with a niggling sense that something isn't right or, as it did in my case, a desire to do something that feels misaligned with our personality.

Embracing sensitivity: Aisling's story

From the time she was little, Aisling knew she was different. Introverted, sensitive and creative, she felt things more deeply than most of her friends. As a young person she loved art, sewing, philosophy and poetry. Not knowing how to combine her passions into a career, she took the advice of a counsellor at school and enrolled in a media course at university.

Several years after completing her degree, she found what seemed like a dream role for a creative young woman – selling media at a leading fashion magazine. Believing she had found a way to combine her love of creativity with her media studies, Aisling was committed to giving this role her best. Her introversion and sensitivity gave her an edge in building relationships. She listened well and had an aesthetic appreciation that her clients greatly valued. After two years of hard work, Aisling's sales results outshone all of her peers. Stylishly dressed and with bonus payments that allowed her to travel and buy herself a new car, it seemed that she had achieved an incredible level of success.

But Aisling felt increasingly hollow. Drained by the energy her role and her clients required of her, her weekends were often spent alone, scrolling mindlessly through social media, binge watching television series or shopping online for another piece of clothing.

When she eventually reached out to me, Aisling suspected she might be depressed. 'Tell me what you enjoy about your role,' I prompted. There was a long pause before she said, 'I thought I loved fashion but I've come to feel that I'm just selling things to people that they don't really need. I feel guilty for not enjoying my role when I know others would be so grateful to have a job like this, but the truth is, it feels misaligned with my values. And I know it might seem idealistic to say this, but I want a role that has meaning.'

Aisling was like many of my clients in telling herself she *should* love her role. While gratitude is an excellent practice that helps balance the negative bias of the brain, there are times when it moves us away from our truth.

I reassured her that while seeking meaning might seem idealistic to some people, research suggests that it's one of the surest ways to find fulfilment in life. We spoke about her values, passions and strengths, and Aisling realised that while creativity was important to her, selling advertising space in a magazine wasn't the way she wanted to express that value. She loved using her strength of sensitivity to connect with people, to understand and appreciate each individual for who they were and to help them meet their needs.

With this new insight, she enrolled in a part-time counselling course and eventually left the world of fashion to set up what quickly became a flourishing practice where she now works with introverts and sensitive people.

Eventually, the part of us that craves purpose and a connection to something bigger than us gets louder until it cannot be ignored – perhaps culminating in a pivotal moment where we feel compelled to tackle a life-long fear or maybe even a crisis that forces us to pause and ask a question as old as time: *What is all of this for?*

We need to listen to these uncomfortable feelings when they arise, because they are our soul's way of alerting us to a problem. It's how we know when it's time to reconnect with the person we are on a deeper level and find the courage to share that authentic version of ourselves with the world.

Meaning is the force that fuels this courage. It gives us a reason to be brave or bold in our own humble way, compels us to speak up and helps us set boundaries and ask for what we want, even though it might be easier to stay silent. Meaning gives us a reason to be brave enough to make change and to stay the course, when our first attempt fails or when others question our choices. This is why it is the first and most crucial element in the journey to building confidence.

FIVE

Our need to find meaning isn't new

The human need to find meaning and examine our place in this unpredictable and unknowable universe is as old as our species. It's the reason every culture has some version of a creation story. In the ancient world, people lived within moral frameworks dictated by whichever gods or goddesses their culture worshipped. When organised religion stepped in, it expanded on these established moral frameworks and wove them into religious stories.

Though still prevalent in many cultures, organised religion is no longer the central tenet of Western civilisation. However, the foundational elements of religion – connecting to the best version of ourselves, being part of a community with shared values – can provide us with a sense of meaning that comes when we experience something larger and more important than ourselves. We all feel a need for belonging, and regular reminders of the human capacity for kindness and compassion. We benefit greatly when we come together in beautiful places to sing, celebrate, grieve or reflect in unison. And while beauty and creativity might feel 'nice to have' but not essential for survival, for as long as humans have been alive, it's the art, stories and rituals we've shared that have given us something solid to believe in.

Another thing the religious world has done far more effectively than the secular one has been to create a framework for spiritual and moral check-ins. Most religious calendars include holidays and holy days that require believers to reflect, atone or celebrate. In the secular world, however, there's no god holding people accountable and the spiritual leaders guiding us to be 'better' versions of ourselves come in many forms. In the absence of a shared framework, it's easy to forget to slow down and seek moments of quiet where we can attune to our inner guidance, and reflect on what gives our life meaning and how we matter as individuals.

Research tells us that having a spiritual life can help protect us from anxiety and depression as well as giving our lives greater meaning. Someone who self-identifies as having a meaningful spiritual life is 80 per cent less likely to become addicted to drugs or alcohol than someone who reports not having a meaningful spiritual life.

Organised religion does a good job of answering the very human need for meaning and connection – things we crave at the deepest level – but this need can be well satisfied outside of organised religion, too. We feel it when we sing with other people in a choir or at a music concert and we sense it when we dance or move together in unison. You might also feel it when you cheer your team on at a soccer match or when you connect with beautifully crafted prose at a poetry reading.

In my own little village on the Mornington Peninsula, a group of women who call themselves The Sea Wolves achieve this in a spectacular way. Formed by a group of four friends during the spring of 2020 in the midst of Victoria's ongoing lockdowns, The Sea Wolves would come together at dawn to swim. Over time, they formed a new ritual. In the dim morning light, in rain, hail or shine, they walk into the icy waters of the bay, hold hands in a circle before 'howling' together like wolves.

One of the founding members of the group (which now includes over 50 women), describes the experience as 'quite spiritual'. They howl to mark birthdays, anniversaries of loss and they've howled for the women of Afghanistan.

New friendships have formed and the women support one another outside of their mornings in the sea. When someone is sick, they take the person food and offer wishes and prayers for healing in the cool morning waters.

Like all shared spiritual experiences, within this simple daily ritual, The Sea Wolves women find joy, connection and healing. In the written words of one group member who has been part of the group for two years, *I've found a sense of belonging and support I never knew I needed. These amazing women give me strength and courage.'*

SIX

Searching for meaning in all the wrong places

Modern marketers teach us that fulfilment can be found from a different set of 'gods', such as achievement, power, beauty, wealth, fame, entertainment, and the perpetual desire to remain youthful. We work hard to make enough money to reward ourselves at shopping malls, luxurious travel destinations, glamorous bars and restaurants. While satisfying in the short term, these pleasures only have a temporary impact on our happiness, and over time, they can leave us feeling pretty empty.

We might fall in love, buy a new car, achieve a promotion or renovate our house, but within months (or if we're lucky, maybe a year), we'll adapt to this change and, because it's no longer novel, the delight we initially felt will fade.

This concept is particularly relevant to activities and possessions that researchers call the 'pleasures'. Martin Seligman, sometimes referred to as 'the father of positive psychology', defines these pleasures as experiences that include a sensory or emotional element, or provide us with a thrill, a sense of exuberance or delight. While they are an important part of life and can certainly lift our mood in the short term, we get used to life's pleasures pretty quickly.

Seligman also researched what he calls 'gratifications' – activities that move us into a state of 'flow' where we are at one with what we're doing and likely to lose all sense of time. This state energises us, and we're most likely to slip into it when participating in activities that engage our innate strengths (more on this in Part Two: Connection). Unlike pleasures, the more we engage in gratifications, the more we enjoy them over time. Ultimately, these activities provide a more profound sense of meaning and fulfilment.

Unfortunately, for many of us, the pull of pleasures is far more alluring than the desire to do the more challenging work of identifying and playing to our strengths.

SEVEN

You are free to choose meaning

'He who has a *why* to live for can bear almost any *how*.'

Friedrich Nietzsche, German philosopher and poet

Between 1942 and 1945, Austrian psychiatrist Viktor Frankl embodied this Nietzsche quote and used it to help him survive the most horrifying years of his life. In the three years that Frankl was shunted between four prisons in the Nazi concentration camp system, he – along with millions of his fellow European Jews – witnessed the worst of humanity.

Surrounded by death and misery, Frankl sustained his inner strength by thinking of his young wife, Tilly, and nurturing the hope that they'd be reunited. He also found meaning in the things he was learning about the human condition – psychological lessons that he hoped to be able to share with the world once the war was over.

When his fellow prisoners teetered on the edge of madness or despair, Frankl observed that the only way to pull them back from the brink was to remind them of their *why*. It didn't matter if this was a lover, family member or their life's work; it only mattered that it existed. Without it, the men could lose the will to live. They might wake up one morning and refuse to get up or go to work, and once a person had reached this point, Frankl observed that nothing – not threats or violence – could make them move. They'd lie on the wet straw, perhaps smoke a cigarette and slowly succumb. Within 48 hours, they'd be dead. American troops noticed a similar pattern of behaviour among traumatised soldiers, and they called it 'give-up-itis'.

Though Frankl and Tilly were never reunited – she died before the end of the war – he did realise his goal of sharing the lessons he'd learned with the world. His wartime experiences cemented his belief that the greatest quest in a human's life was not for power or pleasure, as other psychiatrists of his era theorised, but for *meaning*. His book, *Man's Search for Meaning*, recounts his experiences inside the camps and outlines the concept of logotherapy (from the Greek word for meaning, *logos*), a therapeutic approach he developed based on three fundamental tenets:

1. Life has meaning under all circumstances, even the most miserable ones.
2. Our main motivation for living is our will to find meaning in life.
3. We have freedom to find meaning in what we do and what we experience, or at least in the stance we take when faced with a situation of unchangeable suffering.

Central to logotherapy is the third tenet: nobody can take away another person's freedom to determine their attitude or find meaning in the things they do. However, for a positive attitude to exist, a person must first be able to find meaning in their life. Frankl explains that telling a person to be happy or optimistic is not enough. They must have a reason to be happy (their 'why').

If we extend this line of thinking a little further and apply it to confidence, it becomes clear why finding meaning is the first step towards embodying quiet confidence. *Telling* yourself to be confident will never be enough to make you feel that way. However, if you have a compelling reason behind the desire to increase your confidence, you've found the missing piece of the puzzle.

Meaning has the power to spark authentic courage. It helps us to build trust in ourselves and anchors our actions in a deeper motivation. Without it, the grounded, self-assured confidence we aspire to cannot exist.

First, though, you have to uncover what meaning looks like for you.

EIGHT

Mindful awareness is your greatest tool

No matter where you are on your life's journey or how far away you feel from the quietly confident version of yourself you'd love to be, a greater sense of fulfilment can be found immediately by changing your relationship with your limiting thoughts and difficult feelings, and choosing to live in alignment with your values.

The mindfulness-based therapy Acceptance and Commitment Therapy (ACT) helps us create a kind of 'psychological flexibility' by inviting us to bring awareness to – and make peace with – our difficult internal experiences, while also emphasising that we can find fulfilment in the everyday by acting in alignment with our core personal values.

The philosophy of ACT is that it's counterproductive to try to control difficult emotions and trying to suppress them only leads to greater distress. ACT promotes the view that our negative emotions don't need to be 'fixed or managed or changed' and that there are far more effective ways to alter how you think. Instead, it recommends mindful acceptance as we commit to behaviours that align with our values.

Developing moment-by-moment awareness allows us to tune in and pay attention to what we're experiencing internally. When we're mindfully aware, we're able to pay attention to the uncomfortable (and often inevitable) thoughts and feelings that accompany an experience such as confidence building. When we recognise these feelings, we can make a conscious decision about how we want to interact with them.

It's human nature to want to avoid the discomfort that accompanies negative thoughts and feelings, but when we make room for them rather than exaggerating or ignoring them, we usually discover that we have the potential to change how we relate to these experiences and, in turn, how we relate to ourselves. With this greater sense of internal freedom, we can cultivate lasting change within ourselves and our lives.

This kind of mindful awareness gives us choice, and choice gives us an opportunity to *act* in line with our values, regardless of what our minds are saying. Even when we're experiencing internal difficulty, we have the choice and the power to live a meaningful and purposeful life by taking small steps that align with our values. While we cannot control external situations or events, we *can* control how we respond to those events and contextualise them in the larger story of our lives.

Your values are the key to finding meaning

'Values' are the things that matter the most to you; they are the building blocks that support a meaningful life. A life constructed around values is likely to have meaning *and* be more fulfilling.

Think of your values as the guiding principles by which you want to live. They act as an ongoing compass for your actions. You might consider them to be the guideposts that keep you on track as you move towards your goals. Regardless of whether or not you achieve your goals, aligning with your values as you work towards those goals helps you to feel a greater sense of integrity and self-belief.

Acting decisively and confidently becomes easier when you benchmark decisions against your values. For example, if you've identified 'freedom' as one of your values, this might give you the courage to negotiate a nine-day fortnight when applying for a new role, even in the face of self-doubt. A value of 'wisdom' might provide the confidence you need to return to study, and a value of 'connection' might be the invitation to be more open and vulnerable with a loved one.

As well as providing a benchmark for your larger life decisions – like where you live or whether or not you want to become a parent – your values can also guide smaller decisions in everyday life. Recognising the value of 'health', for example, might provide the impetus for making time for a daily walk or a weekly Pilates class. A value of 'integrity' might encourage an honest conversation when your natural inclination is to avoid conflict.

You will also gain a better understanding of where you feel compromised in life after identifying your values. They can help with boundary-setting in relationships, motivate you to move away from negative situations or give you the courage to speak up when you might otherwise prefer to be silent.

Aligning with your values will be imperfect

Once you are aware of your values, you'll likely find that living fully in alignment with all of them at the same time is difficult. We're almost always moving towards or away from a sense of balance in life and drifting towards those two riverbanks of chaos or rigidity that Dr Dan Siegel describes. This is also true of how we align with our chosen values.

On pages 82–3 you'll find a list of commonly identified values, and you may find, for example, that while working hard on a new project, you are very aligned with the value of 'achievement', but your values of 'health' or 'friendship' are impacted. If you choose to dial down the pressure at work, your value of 'achievement' may decrease, but 'inner harmony' might be improved.

While many values remain with you for life, not all will be static throughout your lifetime. A value such as 'integrity' may never alter, but the value of 'freedom' might become less important when you start a family. The value of 'achievement' might be essential as you establish your career but less critical as you approach retirement. This is why it can be helpful to revisit the values exercise in the next section every few months or at least once each year.

Identifying your values

The key to making this exercise impactful is to put aside thoughts of what others expect of you and ask yourself, 'What really matters to me?' According to Stanford professor Kelly McGonigal, writing about your values is 'one of the most effective psychological interventions ever studied'. Her research showed that the immediate impact of this exercise was that people felt more loving, connected and empathetic, and, at the same time, prouder, more in control and stronger. In the long term, those who wrote about their values experienced improvements in both mental and physical health, including weight loss as well as a reduction in smoking and drinking. As McGonigal says, 'In many cases, these benefits are a result of a one-time mindset intervention. People who write about their values once, for ten minutes, show benefits months or even years later.'

Values exercise

1. From the words on the following pages, select between 10 and 12 values that represent how you want to live right now (add your own words if something is missing).

2. Choose one of your core values and write about it for ten minutes. Write about why this value matters to you and how you have recently expressed or neglected it. Reflect on how the value has helped you in your life. If you have time, you may like to repeat this exercise for some of the other core values.

3. Evaluate your current alignment with your values by scoring them out of 10. For example, a score of 8 will mean you're living in alignment with this value, while a score of 2 means you are neglecting this value.

4. As best as you can, group the values together so you can name your top three core personal values. For example, you might decide that the value of 'connection' encompasses other values you listed, such as compassion, caring, cooperation and kindness. A value of 'integrity' might include honesty, fairness, loyalty and

living sustainably. Memorising your shortlist of values will make it easier for you to benchmark decisions against them, ensuring you're living a life that is meaningful to you.

5. Review your lower-scoring values and note one or two small action steps you can complete in the coming few days to align with them. For example, if your score against 'curiosity' is low, you might choose to research a new concept or ask a question when you're introduced to something you don't know. To align more closely with the value of 'inner harmony', you might engage in a brief daily relaxation practice.

Choose your values

Abundance	Challenge	Engagement	Grace
Acceptance	Cheerfulness	Environment	Gratitude
Achievement	Collaboration	Equality	Growth
Adventure	Community	Ethics	Harmony
Advocacy	Compassion	Excellence	Health
Aesthetic	Competition	Excitement	Helping others
Affection	Connection	Fairness	Honesty
Appreciation	Contribution	Fame	Humanitarianism
Assertiveness	Cooperation	Family	Humility
Authenticity	Courage	Flexibility	Humour
Autonomy	Creativity	Forgiveness	Inclusiveness
Balance	Curiosity	Freedom	Independence
Belonging	Economic	Friendliness	Inner harmony
Boldness	security	Friendship	Innovation
Calmness	Empathy	Fun	Integrity
Caring	Encouragement	Generosity	Intellect

Intimacy	Optimism	Respect/	Spirituality
Joy	Order	self-respect	Status
Justice	Peace	Responsibility	Supportiveness
Kindness	Persistence	Safety	Sustainability
Knowledge	Personal	Security	Time freedom
Leadership	development	Self-care	Tolerance
Learning	Playfulness	Sensuality	Tradition
Love	Pleasure	Serenity	Tranquillity
Loyalty	Popularity	Simplicity	Trust
Meaning	Prosperity	Skilfulness	Wealth
Mindfulness	Purpose	Social	Wisdom
Open-	Recognition	engagement	Work ethic
mindedness	Resilience	Solitude	

Confidence as a value

In the context of this book, we're looking at quiet confidence as a malleable quality or trait we can embody, cultivate and nurture. However, confidence can also be viewed as a value rather than something you must wait to build. This means you can choose to live in alignment with the value of confidence at any time through your immediate actions.

For example, a person who has struggled with feeling confident might feel anxious about walking into a party where they don't know many people. Rather than avoid those feelings, they can decide to act in alignment with their value of confidence even if some anxiety is present. The key to using confidence as a value is being clear about what living in alignment with it looks like for you. For the partygoer, it might mean introducing herself to two strangers, asking someone a question about themselves or bringing other values such as curiosity or kindness into every interaction to make those encounters more meaningful.

A colleague of mine, psychologist and ACT specialist Dr Carrie Hayward, considers confidence as a value when giving a speech. Like many, she finds public speaking a nerve-racking experience. But rather than focusing on what she is feeling or what eventuates, what matters is behaving in a way that aligns with her value of confidence. Sharing information she cares about is purposeful to her, so she aims to feel good about the experience of doing this regardless of how well she performs or whether she stumbles over a word, or how nervous she feels inside.

Consider whether adding confidence to your set of values might allow you to focus on living in alignment with confidence through your immediate *behaviour* rather than confidence being about how you think or feel about your ability to do something.

Apply kaizen to uncover your values

As we explored earlier, kaizen – the philosophy of implementing small, continuous changes over the long term to elicit dramatic positive change – can also be a wonderful self-development tool. In this exercise, we're going to apply a kaizen technique known as 'the five questions' to delve deeper into where meaning might be hiding in some of your memories. When trying to get to the root of a problem, kaizen asks the question 'why?' five times in succession. The logic behind this technique is that each answer brings you closer to the truth or root problem you are trying to uncover. Here's how it might work in practice.

Recall a time when you didn't feel confident or 'in your element'.

When you settle on a strong memory, write it down in a journal or notebook and include as many details about the experience as possible.

For example: *I felt uncomfortable after gossiping with some of my work colleagues. Three of us were sitting together at lunch when Pip lowered her voice and said that she didn't think James (our new team member) was up to the job. I was surprised by this because James's work was good and he seemed really nice and eager to learn. But Brian agreed with Pip and started making fun of the way James talked when he was on the phone with clients. 'Does that bother you since his desk is next to yours?' asked Pip. 'Oh, yeah,' I replied. 'It's impossible to concentrate when he's on a call. It's very distracting.' The two of them continued the conversation, and it got progressively meaner. I found myself wishing I hadn't said anything at all.*

Q1. *Why* did this experience make me feel ill at ease?

A1. I like my work colleagues and enjoy spending time with them, but this interaction felt different. I left feeling uncomfortable and drained.

Q2: *Why?*

A2: Because even though it's not my style to gossip, I found myself chiming in.

Q3: *Why?*

A3: When I'm in a group setting like this, I feel a sense of pressure to belong, and occasionally, I go against my core values in order to fit in.

Q4: *Why?*

Q4: I want to be liked and included in the group. But this encounter has highlighted that gossiping leaves me feeling far worse than the benefit of belonging.

Q5: *Why?*

A5: Gossip or speaking about anyone badly conflicts with my values of loyalty and integrity. Next time, I will find the courage to speak up and suggest to my colleagues that speaking to that person directly would be better.

The memory this person has chosen, along with the answers they've given, suggests that as well as the values of loyalty and integrity, authenticity and belonging are other values that are important to them. As is evident from this exercise, there will be times when your values conflict with one another. Reflecting like this can help provide a clearer understanding of which values you prioritise more highly and how you might change your behaviour to feel more aligned with them.

Uncovering values through crisis: Mei's story

Mei came to see me because she had recently become more connected to her values but was having difficulty finding a role that aligned with them. She had returned to Australia after several years in the US and enrolled in a health-coaching course in the hope that it would lead to a more meaningful career. Before this, she'd held a senior position at a global finance company in New York City, handling high-profile clients. At the time, this had felt like her dream job, but a freak accident in the city caused her to rethink everything.

On the way to an appointment, Mei had stepped on a broken subway grate. A long metal rod snapped off the grate, slipped under her sandal and became impaled through the centre of her foot.

Although the accident was horrific and left Mei in shock, her overall memory of that afternoon isn't all negative.

In the seconds after the accident, strangers on the street stopped to help her. People came rushing out of nearby buildings to comfort her, call an ambulance, stop the bleeding and stay with her until the paramedics arrived. Once at the hospital, she continued to encounter kindness from every person who cared for her, something she'd not been used to in the often disconnected, fast-paced life in the city.

This experience of being so cared for in such a vulnerable moment had touched Mei. It revealed something she hadn't been aware of: she valued kindness, empathy, compassion and connection far more than she had previously acknowledged. After gaining this insight, she decided she wanted to live a life more aligned with those values. She decided that working in the often-competitive field of finance felt meaningless when compared with the work of the paramedics and healthcare professionals who had just helped her.

A few months later, while enjoying the content in her health course, Mei was starting to feel uneasy. She could see that while a career in health might align with her values, it wasn't a role that energised her. After practising with clients as part of her course requirements, Mei realised she might not be cut out for listening to adverse health stories on a daily basis. If she was honest with herself, she found these conversations quite draining.

After exploring her career choices with me in a little more depth, Mei came to recognise that it was possible to engage her values and strengths in her previous role in a more purposeful way. She just needed to look at things a little differently.

Eventually, she dropped out of her course and returned to the career she excelled in. Her new focus became leading her team with the values of empathy, compassion and kindness. She's now less focused on being competitive than she was previously (something that had always drained her) and she prioritises connection with her colleagues and clients. As well as feeling more energised and inspired by her role, Mei's authentic approach has begun to garner new recognition, her team is excelling in their performance and her sales results are better than ever.

Magic happens when values meet strengths

Mei's story is a wonderful example of how important it is to stay open and flexible as you work out the best way to live your values. Identifying them is a crucial first step to finding meaning in life, but being aware of your values doesn't mean you will always land on the right path right away.

You may take a few wrong turns at first, as I did in the early days of my business. If you find this to be the case, you may need to prioritise different values or find a way of embracing your values that's a better fit.

Two years after retraining as a coach, my business began to flourish. I hired a business coach who encouraged me to embrace the values of achievement and growth, even though these weren't inherently top priorities for me. 'You don't have a business at all,' he told me. 'You've just bought yourself a job. A true business-woman would want to inspire others by being highly successful in business.' He suggested that if I was serious about my work,

I needed to embrace my success and grow my business into something bigger. Not trusting the intuitive resistance within me, I took his advice and rented office space in Melbourne's CBD, then hired my first contractors.

With his support, I found leadership coaching contracts with corporate clients, charged higher fees and watched my business steadily grow. But after ticking all of those boxes in just a short space of time, I realised that the business I was growing was leaving me increasingly unfulfilled. The daily demands of managing a growing team and hustling to acquire bigger contracts meant I was doing less of the work that felt meaningful to me – working directly with clients.

That niggling feeling in the pit of my stomach told me that the values my well-intentioned mentor had pushed me towards weren't the ones I hold most dear. So I allowed myself to trust my intuition and put aside my ego as I decided to downsize my business. I let go of my contractors and my city premises and took my business back home.

As much as I loved the idea of inspiring others through achievement, I realised I valued other things so much more. I wanted to spend my working hours directly with clients, and I wanted more time with my family. I loved working from the comfort of my living room, and dropping my fees allowed me to continue working with creative clients. I was also able to shed the stressful tasks that weren't adding value to my life. While my business looked less impressive to the outside world and my income halved, I was once again living in alignment with my true personal values and making more of my natural strengths.

As Mei and I discovered, things click into place when we can link what is meaningful with what we do well. A meaningful life is often a by-product of this combination. In Part Two of the book, we'll look at combining the values you've identified in this part of the book with your natural strengths.

Living your values can help you achieve goals

Acceptance and Commitment Therapy (see page 77) approaches goals and values as two very different things. Goals can be big or small, and once set, they point us in a chosen direction and give us something to work towards. Very often, however, we don't have total control over whether or not we achieve our goals, and they might take months or years to accomplish.

Living in alignment with your values, on the other hand, is within our control, and for many of the introverted clients I work with, a values-based focus is more appealing. Living to our values is something we can action immediately. Meaning can be found when we are true to our values while working towards a goal – not in achieving the goal itself. To illustrate this, my colleague Carrie offers the following example:

> 'Let's say my goal is to publish a book. If I do manage to get a book deal, I probably won't have full control over details such as when the book will get published, who prints it, where it goes on sale or how well it sells. I can't control the outcome. However, the meaning in this experience will be found in me living my values of creativity, sharing knowledge and being courageous.

If I stay aligned with those values and give them my attention, rather than focusing on the outcome, the book will take care of itself. And I won't have to wait until it's published to find meaning in the experience because the process of moving towards the goal will have been meaningful.'

Similarly, you might sit down at your desk in the morning with the smaller goal of filing your taxes that day. If you get to 6 pm and this task isn't completed because you diverted your attention to comforting a friend or spending time with your partner, the day won't have been a failure because you still spent it living in alignment with one of your values. You may not have achieved your initial goal, but you can go to bed with the knowledge that your day still had meaning.

Set goals that align with your values

Revisit the exercise you completed on page 8 (in the introduction). Re-read the list of things you dream about doing and the areas you'd like to improve and keep these in mind as you write out a handful of goals. If, like some of my clients, you feel some resistance to goal-setting, choose just a couple of goals that are meaningful for you.

When choosing your goals, make sure they are realistic *and* specific. While somewhat overused, the SMART acronym (specific, measurable, achievable, realistic and timebound) is simple, and it provides an excellent framework for creating goals. (An internet search of this term will provide plenty of detailed information on how to apply this to goal-setting.) Beyond this, make sure you link your goals to your existing values because this will deepen your connection to them.

If you feel inclined to set big ambitious goals, make sure you're not including them to impress other people or because you feel that they are what society is asking of you. Align them to what's most important to you.

Set up the possibility of a positive feedback loop by including some small, achievable goals on your list. Once we achieve a few easy milestones, we start seeing ourselves in a different light – as courageous people who dare to go after what they want – and we begin to build trust in ourselves, which is key for confidence building.

Don't be put off by including goals you perceive as being somewhat outside your control, such as meeting a loving life-partner. While the outcome is less easily managed than a tangible goal such as saving enough for an overseas trip, the reality is that without investing some energy, your goal has little chance of ever being realised.

Write it down, then tell a friend

Write it down: According to a 2015 study, those who write their goals down are 42 per cent more likely to achieve them than those who simply think about them.

One of the reasons for this is that the action of writing triggers encoding – a biological process where the things we perceive are transported to our brain's hippocampus for analysis, making it much more likely we'll remember them. Another reason this works is that writing a goal down encourages us to strategise about how we're going to achieve it.

Importantly, goals should be written and described as vividly as possible (if you want to supplement these descriptions with pictures, photos or images that further crystallise this vision, even better).

Add accountability for better results: The likelihood of achieving a goal jumps to 62 per cent for those who do all of the above steps and *also* tell a supportive friend about these commitments. Incredibly, it jumps to a whopping 76 per cent for those who do all of the above *and* send a weekly update on their progress to a friend. If you struggle with following through on the goals you set for yourself, these easy strategies will improve your chances of success.

If you don't feel ready to set specific goals at this point, focus instead on aligning your actions with the kind of person you aspire to be – not an extrovert or someone with different talents and qualities, but rather the best possible version of *yourself*. You can move towards this version of yourself by building small habits that compound over time. This will not only move you towards goals you may not even realise you have, but it will also put you in a better position to achieve your goals once they do come into focus. Try the following exercise to get you started.

Your best possible self

1. **What does your best self look like?**

   What does your best self look like? A good friend? Loving sibling, partner or mother? Prolific artist? Write a brief list describing the person you aspire to be.

2. **What sort of things would this 'best self' do?**

   For each descriptor on your list, brainstorm one or more actions that a person like this might undertake every day. For example, a good friend, loving sibling or partner might send encouraging or thoughtful text messages regularly. A loving mother might prioritise reading a book with their child each night. A prolific artist might commit to painting for two hours each morning.

3. **Choose one of these actions and run with it.**

   Now, circle one of these actions. It should be something simple that you could undertake tomorrow. If you aspire to be a healthier person, the action you circle might be 'walking 10,000 steps'. However, if you feel resistance to that idea, make it smaller – perhaps 2000 steps – until the feeling of resistance goes away.

   Once you've decided on the action, commit to doing it each day for the next few days, and attach this new habit to a habit you already do automatically – this is what *Atomic Habits* author James Clear refers to as 'habit stacking'. In this case, it might involve leaving your car at home and walking 2000 steps to the local coffee shop you already visit each morning.

Going after big and small goals at the same time: Ben's story

Ben recently discovered that one of his core values is 'creativity'. As a child, he spent most of his free time sketching and playing music, but now he devotes no time to undertaking these activities. He has realised that his unhappiness at work (he is assistant manager to the CEO of a security company) is partly a result of being so disconnected from his value of creativity. Because of this, Ben has set one big goal and one smaller goal that align with this value.

His big goal is to find a new job in the next six months and his smaller goal is to do something creative several times a week.

For his big goal, Ben has set his sights on looking for a similar role in a more creative environment where he can be closer to ideas, people and projects that connect with his value of creativity. He has broken this big goal into smaller steps (connecting with people on LinkedIn, having coffees with colleagues in creative businesses and updating his CV with transferable skills) and he will work through each of these in the coming weeks and months.

For his smaller goal, he has decided to carve out time to play guitar at least three times a week this month. He has taken action already by buying new sheet music and reaching out to a musician friend to set up a regular jamming session.

NINE

The importance of understanding our stories

Our life's path is built upon stories – thousands of them, in varying layers of influence and importance. Good or bad, everything that happens to us becomes another element in our larger life narrative. The words we use to retell an experience – first, for ourselves, and later, to others – reveal a huge amount about how we see individual events *and* ourselves.

Story is so crucial to our species that an entire field of psychology emerged around it in the late 1970s. The field of narrative psychology studies how we use story to understand experiences and our very identity. And as with any decent novel, movie, play or musical, meaning is essential to story. Without it, there's nothing to motivate the main character, provide interest or give the narrative direction. A story without meaning is aimless, and personal story is no different.

Being able to link the events of your life together in a way that helps you derive meaning from them, as Viktor Frankl did, increases the likelihood that you'll have a more positive view of your future and yourself. If a person continues to tell a story about how they're always unlucky or destined to fail, they probably won't feel great about themselves or their prospects. Narrative therapy provides the opportunity to externalise and deconstruct our stories so we might recognise our inner strength as well as our capacity for overcoming adversity.

Research from narrative psychologists also shows that our sense of wellbeing is directly tied to the stories we tell about ourselves. When we explore our stories and reflect on their meaning, we also have the opportunity to change the narrative. Even failure narratives can have a powerful positive impact when we choose to tell them in a different way.

Mei's story might have been one of failure if she had chosen to tell it that way, but instead, it's a story of courage and self-awareness. Dropping out of her health coaching course meant that she had wasted some time and money but the experience was also invaluable. Only by reflecting on what wasn't inherently right for her could she pinpoint her most important values and strengths.

We learn about ourselves through our stories, and they allow us to recognise our innate capacity for growth. When we externalise and deconstruct our stories, we can tell them differently. Our revised stories make it possible to give ourselves credit for overcoming challenges, and in turn, we can appreciate ourselves in new ways. We learn about our resilience and come to see that we have the capacity to deal with new challenges in the future.

Sharing our stories with others also has its benefits. Storytelling boosts empathy, deepens connection, and can even produce the hormone oxytocin in the brain – the hormone that increases the bond between a mother and baby. While the thought of sharing your story with someone else may leave you feeling vulnerable, it's also a powerful way to help you heal and grow. Perhaps this is why Susan Cain says the single, most important question you can ask yourself is, *What narrative have I constructed from the events of my life?*

What story are you telling?

Spend time reflecting on the life story you've been telling yourself and others. You may even like to complete the following 'My life story' exercise below. It's a narrative therapy tool used in positive psychology and can be incredibly revealing. If you've experienced trauma, this exercise is best worked through with a qualified therapist.

My life story

Write your life story in the third person, casting yourself as the hero, not the victim. The aim of this exercise isn't to fixate on specific memories but to detach from your history enough that you get a broader view of your life and create a life outline that emphasises pivotal moments of growth and intensity.

1. Give your story a title. This could be as simple as 'Mei's life story' or more descriptive, perhaps capturing a core theme in your life, e.g., 'Mei: A values-led life'.
2. Create seven chapter titles of up to ten words, each representing a significant life stage or event. Beside each chapter title, write a single sentence summarising its essence. Again, this should be

in the third person. For instance, next to a chapter titled 'No direction' you might write: 'Her teenage years were filled with insecurity and confusion.'

3. Once you've completed the chapter titles of your story, include a final chapter where you describe your future life in detail. What aspirations are you working towards? Who do you want to be? Describe this quietly confident version of yourself, and as you detail your hopes and dreams, don't be held back by a scarcity mindset or fear.

4. Review your story and add any content that helps you make sense of your narrative.

I found the experience of completing this exercise surprisingly liberating and healing. Writing out my story helped me structure my thoughts about my life and better understand the events that have shaped me most. It also helped me to recognise that some of the most difficult moments in my life were the ones that provided the most meaning.

Our life experiences influence us, but they need not dictate our identity. Experiences are opportunities to build resilience and courage, deepen our capacity for empathy and understanding, and they can offer the most meaningful learnings.

Identity is forged in the fire

In a discussion with Pico Iyer on the wonderful podcast *On Being*, Elizabeth Gilbert describes an exercise her friend Rob Bell uses to help people uncover the lessons in their suffering. He asks them to imagine two whiteboards. The one on the left includes all of their negative experiences: professional failures, a painful divorce, addiction, or the death of a loved one, for example. The board on the right includes positive experiences: falling in love, the birth of a child, friendships and adventures.

We all want lives that are filled with experiences from the whiteboard on the right, and we want that for our loved ones, too. But Rob found that when asked to pick the three events that made them into the people they needed to become, most people pointed to the experiences on the other board and said it's the misfortune, the loss, the failure, the addiction that most shaped them.

Though we may never be able to say we are glad for those experiences, Gilbert says we can still recognise that 'something interesting is happening here. You are growing into something more subtle, more elegant, more kind, more human than you might have been without it – certainly, more capable of empathy.'

I know this to be true of my own experience, and I've also seen it many times over with clients and with members of my family. While it's undeniable that we find meaning in life's joyous moments, such as the enduring love we feel with a partner, the birth of a child, or the wonder we experience when travelling to new places, research supports the idea that what doesn't kill us makes us stronger.

Psychologists Richard Tedeschi and Lawrence Calhoun Tedeschi found that post-traumatic growth often happens naturally, but is best supported when we have what they call 'expert companions' such as friends, family or professionals willing to listen to our stories. The process of reliving the guilt, shame, grief, fear or confusion we've experienced can help us piece together the puzzle of a traumatic experience in a way that helps shape a new narrative. As we do this, we may come to appreciate paradoxes such as this one: In loss, there is gain, and in vulnerability, we find strength.

Our negative experiences can also help us recognise how resilient we are and offer opportunities to rethink ourselves and our worlds. They can teach us to regulate our emotions more effectively, improve our relationships with others and give us a greater appreciation for life. In some instances, they can even lead to spiritual growth.

Researchers estimate that between half to two-thirds of all trauma survivors experience post-traumatic growth, and the key differentiator between those who grow and those who don't is mindset. Your ability to move forward from adversity rests largely on your ability to create a positive reinterpretation of the experience, feel optimistic about the future and cultivate an enduring sense of acceptance. In other words, to move forward you must understand what you can take from that experience into your future or what gives your life experience *meaning*.

Reframe your stories to better serve you

Pay attention to the stories you've been telling yourself and others. If you recently had a break-up, did you consider that to be proof that you're unlovable? Or did it free you up to find a partner who will love you for being the most authentic version of you? If you lost a job, did that mean you weren't valued? Or was it an unexpected opportunity to try your hand at something you suspect will be more fulfilling?

Think of a difficult experience you've faced recently.

How have you framed that event in your mind?

How have you told that story to your family or friends?

What does that story say about you as a person?

Are there beliefs you have about the person you were in that story that you're now ready to let go of?

Can you reframe this event in a way that is still honest but more positive and meaningful?

Consider how this story might be the launchpad for a new way of being in your life.

Bonus mindset exercise

A nice add-on to this exercise is to write a list of all the people who have been good to you in some way. Our negativity bias means we're sometimes more inclined to think of those who have wronged, shamed or hurt us. Not only can this make us feel isolated, it can also deplete our confidence and shake our faith in humanity.

Reflecting on the many people who have shown you kindness, cheered you up, given you an opportunity or shared their friendship and love with you is an easy way to right this balance and remind yourself of the many positive moments you've shared with other people. As mentioned earlier, the beauty of the human brain is that it's capable of creating new neural pathways where we want them to exist. The more we train our mind to remember and look out for these beautiful moments, the better we'll become at spotting them when they happen.

'Not good enough': Tackling a familiar origin story

Whether you view the narrative arc of your life as a hero's journey, romantic comedy or melodrama, if you're an introvert, the early part of your story likely includes memories of feeling deficient in some way. In my experience, this is an almost universal experience for introverts.

In an enlightening conversation with psychologist Rebecca Ray, author of *Setting Boundaries*, we explored why perfectionism and introversion seem to go hand in hand. For years, I've noticed that most of my introverted clients harbour a belief that they have to be 'good' or 'perfect', and when we scratch the surface of this, the unreasonably high expectations we have of ourselves are almost always linked to a personal narrative of not being good enough in some way.

Ray believes that introverts (she includes herself in this group) begin writing the narrative of 'I'm not good enough' very early in life for two key reasons. The first – as I touched on in the introduction – is that society caters to and rewards the extrovert majority. Consequently, introverts are forced to focus on all the things they are *not* from the moment they engage with society.

As an example, Ray shared a story about her three-year-old son. He looks forward to 'show and tell' at his day care every week. As a budding extrovert, he relishes the chance to stand in front of his classmates and talk about his favourite things. While sitting in on one of his presentations one day, Ray noticed that the shy children in the group refused to take their turn in front of the class. Overwhelmed and clearly anxious at the thought of being called upon, several retreated to the back of the mat, where they watched their outgoing peers soak up the attention and enjoy the praise of the caretakers and other children.

For all the children in the room, this experience wires neural pathways in their brains and shapes a story they'll tell themselves for years to come. Extroverts like Ray's son learn that speaking in front of people is fun and there's nothing to fear, while the quieter children in the back will learn the opposite lesson. For them, speaking in front of people is something to be feared and, more than likely, avoided at all costs. The adults who care for them reward behaviours that don't come naturally to them. In day care, those rewards will include praise, attention and social connection, and later, these will expand to include friendships, invitations, first dates and promotions. It won't be long before the introverted children start wondering things like, *How on earth am I going to be successful when I can't be like that?*

The second reason Ray believes introverts frequently harbour a story of not being good enough is linked to the previous example because it relates to how we are conditioned by the adults in our lives – teachers, caregivers and parents. Some adults do a wonderful job of honouring a child's unique personality and giving them the freedom to shine in their own way. Still, many introverted children are being 'helped' by adults who encourage them to behave differently from how they feel.

A core memory forms when a teacher inadvertently shames a child for not wanting to speak in class or put themselves 'out there' in some way, or a parent gets frustrated because the child won't do something other children are doing. The adult doing the pressuring might be an extrovert who wants the child to behave 'normally' (i.e., like them), but they could also be an introvert who doesn't want the child to experience the same discomforts they did. Either way, the result is the same: the child gets the message that they aren't behaving in a desired way. After these experiences, the brain will look for information confirming this story because this is how we are wired. This is called confirmation bias. Without even realising it, we'll spend the rest of our childhood, adolescence and adulthood so focused on noticing evidence that supports that story of deficiency that we won't even register evidence to the contrary.

Forty thousand years ago, when our brains evolved into the human brains we have today, belonging to a group was integral to survival and the only way to survive in a dangerous and primitive world. Being part of a tribe or community meant having access to resources, information and protection, not to mention a chance to reproduce. Not belonging made a person vulnerable to being shunned or maybe even killed. Consequently, fitting in became one of our most important survival skills – and our brains still train us to want to behave this way.

When a little person sees evidence that they *aren't* like the rest of a group, this disrupts their sense of belonging and a fearful thought takes hold: *Not only am I defective, I'm different. If I'm different, that means I won't belong.* To avert disaster, the brain plays this thought on a loop so often that it becomes a core belief. The brain wants us to survive, and replaying this fear is its way of begging us to address the crisis: 'Can you please fix yourself? You need to be part of the group because being on the outside is dangerous.'

This was certainly my own experience growing up. Although my family life was pretty stable, my extroverted parents often struggled to understand me. They considered my love of spending time alone reading or wandering the local bush tracks antisocial and somewhat strange. They found my way of viewing the world too deep and overly reflective. I had the sense I wasn't social enough and was regularly called selfish for wanting time on my own. In my teenage years, when I finally pushed myself to spend time with a group of girls because this was what everyone else was doing, my family were relieved to see me acting in a 'normal' way. Not surprisingly, when I reflect on this time, this was one of the unhappiest periods of my life. I was curious to know if Ray had any strategies to help us remedy the story of our perceived deficiency, and her answer was no surprise to me: 'It's one thing we can't fix, and I love telling the truth about that. I have it. You have it. We have it forever.'

I found great comfort in this answer; it reminded me that while sometimes it's important to rewrite our narratives, this needs to be balanced with accepting ourselves, just as we are. The sweet spot between these polarities is something most of us will never quite perfect but self-awareness is key here. As you move in the direction of your goals, continue to ask yourself two questions. 'Does this choice feel really right or true for me?' and 'Am I holding myself back because I'm telling myself a story that no longer serves me?'

The conversation with Ray revealed that while my initial interest in confidence was born from a desire to help my clients, I was also writing this book for a younger version of myself. If I'd known then that my behaviour was entirely normal for an introvert and that my sensitive nature would later be a great asset in my work, I might have been more accepting of myself.

I hope that when you see yourself reflected in these pages, you'll feel a great sense of relief in knowing that you're not alone. It's also my hope that you'll begin to embrace your innate characteristics and value your uniqueness in a whole new way.

Making peace with your story

We can begin our most meaningful work when we make peace with our stories. Rather than expend precious emotional and mental energy trying to rewrite our 'not good enough' story, Ray advises learning not to make too much of that story.

We may not be able to turn our stories off entirely, but we can accept that they will sometimes play out in the background while we work, parent, socialise and date. Ray likens her 'not good enough' story to an unhelpful back-seat driver. It comes along for the ride whether you like it or not. Accepting that it's there makes room for it without allowing it to dictate your behaviour. It can't choose the music on the radio, tell you which road to take or take the wheel to choose your destination.

Rather than fight it, embrace the noise by saying something like, 'Okay, that story is there. I expected it to be there, but I won't let it stop me from giving the world what I've got.' As Frankl learned, we each have the power to choose where we focus our attention and energy. Try to turn your attention to a better, more supportive story.

TEN

You are already making a difference

The Japanese term *ikigai* refers to the concept that each of us has a reason for being. Combining *iki*, which means 'life', and *gai*, which means 'value' or 'worth', *ikigai* helps give our lives a sense of meaning. Héctor García, co-author of the book *Ikigai*, includes it as one of the secrets to the wellbeing of the elderly residents of Okinawa – an area renowned for the incredible longevity of its citizens.

Each of the active seniors García interviewed in Okinawa had a meaningful reason for living: 'When we asked what their *ikigai* was, they gave us explicit answers, such as their friends, gardening, and art. Everyone knows what the source of their zest for life is, and is busily engaged in it every day.'

In Western literature, the approach to identifying a person's *ikigai* is usually visual – in the form of a Venn diagram of four overlapping circles. The idea is that within each circle, you identify:

- what you love doing;
- what you are good at;
- what the world needs; and
- what you can be paid for.

At the very centre, where all four circles overlap, is where you'll find your *ikigai* or purpose. It's worth noting that in García's research of the elderly Okinawans, being paid didn't come into the equation, which might indicate that it's less important to our source of *ikigai* than the previous three categories.

Once you have identified your *ikigai*, consider it your reason for getting up every morning. It is here that you should focus your efforts. This philosophy also suggests that it's helpful to start small (which aligns with the concept of kaizen) and that *ikigai* is most easily achieved when we can find joy in life's small moments, a concept we'll explore in depth in Part Four: Presence.

Find your *ikigai*

Set aside around 30 minutes and add notes into each of the four circles on the *ikigai* diagram.

Write a few sentences about how and where these areas might come together in your personal or professional life to define your *ikigai*.

If you feel that you're not aligned to your *ikigai*, consider a few small steps you can take in the coming week to bring you closer to your purpose.

My take on 'purpose' is very similar to *ikigai*. I believe that our lives are most purposeful when we can find meaning in the everyday and when our experiences make a difference in other people's lives. I have long believed this was the case, yet I struggled to find research that backed this up – until I stumbled across researcher Zach Mercurio's work.

For the past decade, he's been studying what gives our lives purpose and meaning. His emphasis is less on encouraging us to 'find our purpose' and more on considering how we might 'awaken our purpose' and bring it to life daily. As he points out, a popular view is that purpose is reserved for a select few who have the means and the drive to pursue something significant, but in fact, the most inspiring and purpose-driven people are often those doing ordinary things with an extraordinary perspective.

Each of us has a story to tell and every one of us wants to matter. Zach believes that purposeful living is accessible to all of us and we can gain greater clarity about how we are already being purposeful by asking ourselves the following questions:

- What are my innate strengths? (If you're not sure, we'll be exploring this in detail in Part Two: Connection.)
- Where am I already being useful or impacting other people?

At the intersection of these answers, you're likely to see that *you're already making a difference.* But clarifying your *ikigai* or stating your purpose isn't enough to create change. Engaging your purpose through action is what matters, and when you do this regularly, it's likely you'll find that living with a greater sense of purpose immediately inspires more self-belief.

Zach suggests that one of the easiest ways to bring your purpose to life is to look at your calendar each morning and ask yourself not, 'What do I have on today?' but rather, 'How will I make a difference to the people I interact with today?'

I've found this to be one of the simplest ways to create purposeful change in my life, and it's something I have often shared with clients. Like anyone who feels a sense of purpose at work, I have also recognised that while my intention is to make a difference in other people's lives, the people I work with also make the biggest difference in mine. I find my clients endlessly inspiring.

Finding meaning in grief: Carlos's story

While writing this chapter, my client Carlos was grieving the recent loss his father. He told me how a new volunteer role at a palliative care and bereavement support service was bringing new meaning to his life.

Like many people in the midst of grief, Carlos found it difficult to be social and he found that many of his friends were uneasy with his grief. Wanting to save both them and himself from moments of discomfort, his natural inclination was to withdraw. Volunteering gave him the opportunity to connect with others who understood how he was feeling. 'Sometimes we just sit in silence,' he told me, 'and it doesn't feel at all awkward or strange. It's different to being out with friends where I feel I need to put on a happy face – I feel that this is the only time I can be with other people and allow myself to feel what I'm feeling.'

As well as giving Carlos space to grieve without pressure, spending time at the bereavement centre gave him the chance to offer others the kind of support he would have valued in the difficult months leading up to his dad's death and in the early days of grief. Not only was it a productive way of honouring his dad's memory, it gave Carlos's experience of loss greater meaning.

I've heard many similar stories from other clients. One started a not-for-profit organisation supporting female survivors of family violence after years of watching her mother suffer abuse. Another mentors refugee and migrant women who are starting businesses because her own family has stories of how hard it can be to integrate into a new country.

I've come to realise that when we make a small difference to one person, it has a ripple effect that also changes the lives of the people they're in touch with. It's motivating and confidence-boosting to recognise that we can change the world in our own small ways and that even our very small actions can matter.

Meaning is contagious

If you're not yet sure what your purpose is, take comfort in knowing that it might be waiting to be discovered. This was the case for TOMS founder, Blake Mycoskie, who stumbled across his purpose while on holiday. In 2006, the 29-year-old entrepreneur was in Argentina when he met a fellow American in a Buenos Aires café. When they got talking, she told him she was there on a 'shoe drive' – something Mycoskie had never heard of. She explained that lots of children, even in relatively well-developed countries like Argentina, go without footwear. Not only does that make activities like playing, attending school or getting water from a nearby well much harder, or even impossible, it also makes the children more vulnerable to injury and disease.

Mycoskie was intrigued and accompanied the woman and her team on some of their shoe drops outside of the city. Though he'd known that children sometimes went without shoes, these experiences opened his eyes to the huge life disadvantage this was. 'Now, for the first time, I saw the real effects of being shoeless: the blisters, the sores, the infections.' Charity aid provided a temporary solution, but the supply of shoes wasn't steady and therefore wouldn't change things in the long term.

The entrepreneurial part of his brain started searching for sustainable ways to solve this problem, and thus the idea for TOMS was born. It would be the first company founded on a one-to-one model, where, for every pair of shoes purchased, a pair would be donated to a child in need, ensuring a reliable supply of shoes. They'd call the company Tomorrow's Shoes (which was later shortened to TOMS).

An Argentine friend, Alejo Nitti, was equally passionate about this idea and joined what Mycoskie calls 'the mission'. The two of them set out to find a shoemaker willing to make a more comfortable version of the *alpargata* – classic Argentinian canvas espadrilles – in designs and colours that would appeal to fashion-conscious American consumers. As the shoemaker got to work from his tiny factory, Mycoskie and Nitti sought out artisans to collaborate with on the brightly coloured fabrics and designs they had in mind. When Mycoskie travelled home to continue running his driver's education business, he had 250 pairs of his 'modified *alpargatas*' stuffed inside duffel bags and a purpose fuelling him on.

In his book *Start Something That Matters*, Mycoskie reflects on the early days of TOMS. Though there was no money for flashy marketing campaigns, time and again, the story of the company resonated with people and prompted them to take action. He invited a group of friends over, shared his experiences of being in Argentina and showed them the shoes. They wanted to help and gave Mycoskie a list of stores they thought might be interested. Even better, he said, 'They all left my apartment that night wearing pairs they'd insisted on buying from me.' He took this as a good sign.

When emailing and phoning the stores on the list didn't work, he drove to American Rag, the store at the top of his list, and asked to meet their shoe buyer. Though this woman judged more shoes every month than he could imagine, the purpose behind the brand caught her attention. 'From the beginning, she realised that TOMS was more than just a shoe. It was a story. And the buyer loved the story as much as the shoe – and knew she could sell both of them.'

The message and the mission behind these $40 espadrilles spread like wildfire. When the fashion writer for the *Los Angeles Times* heard about TOMS, they put the story and the shoe on the front page of the *Times'* Calendar section: In that day alone, the existing 900 orders on the website jumped to 2200.

Features in *Vogue, TIME, People, Elle* and *Teen Vogue* followed. National stores Nordstrom and Urban Outfitters ordered stock, and celebrities like Keira Knightley, Scarlett Johansson and Tobey Maguire were photographed wearing TOMS. The purpose Mycoskie stumbled upon in that Argentine café wasn't just powerful, it was also contagious. His mission meant something to the people wearing his shoes. They didn't just like what TOMS stood for, they were proud to wear the shoes and contribute in their own way because *they* found meaning in knowing that their purchase was also caring for a child in another part of the world. Consequently, if someone commented on their footwear, they didn't just say 'thanks', they spread the TOMS message for free – far more effectively than any big-budget ad campaign could have done.

TOMS has since expanded to TOMS eyewear and other apparel. They've helped millions of people in need, and the one-to-one business model Mycoskie created has inspired countless other innovative and socially conscious entrepreneurs.

Meaning summary

- Meaning is the force that fuels courage.
- Research suggests that having a meaningful spiritual life can protect against depression and addiction.
- Your values provide a key to a meaningful life.
- Meaning can also be found by understanding (and possibly reframing) your life story.
- Most people find that a meaningful life involves making a difference in other people's lives.

Part Two

Connection

Knowing the elements that give our lives meaning is the first step in building trust in ourselves. The next is connecting to our natural gifts, to the aspect of our personality that already knows confidence, and connecting to other people. In this part of the book, we'll explore how to build the deeper connections that anchor and support quiet confidence.

The desire for connection is a driving force for all of us, and I've come to believe that our need for it underpins many of the challenges we encounter with confidence. Countless conversations with clients have taught me that we lose confidence most easily when a connection of some sort is broken. This can happen in many ways. We might lose touch with who we are or stop trusting our intuition. A fracture in a relationship or community might set us adrift, or we might lose faith in something bigger than us – nature, politics or our sense of spirituality.

Finding the courage to leave: Hannah's story

At times we lose touch with our own truth, allowing ourselves to be treated disrespectfully and ignoring the warning signs in our bodies. This was the case for Hannah, a senior lawyer who had spent six years working in mergers and acquisitions for a prestigious firm in Melbourne's CBD. She came to see me eight months after the arrival of a new manager when her working life had become incredibly stressful.

Like many of my clients, Hannah was a quiet achiever. Conscientious and thorough, her style had always been to let her good work speak for itself. For some reason, her personality and her approach seemed to rub her new manager up the wrong way.

He created a clique with a couple of her colleagues and Hannah found herself increasingly left off meeting invitations, no longer included in Friday night drinks and rarely given new client briefs.

'I feel like I'm being paranoid,' she told me, 'but something has really shifted.' We spoke about the options that were available to her and Hannah concluded that the only approach she could take was to have a direct conversation with her manager about her desire to take on more work and be included in important meetings. It took a lot of courage to do this, particularly while she was feeling so vulnerable.

Her boss was pleasant in their interaction and feigned surprise at her concerns, which only added to Hannah's confusion. When she reiterated this story a few weeks later, I asked if anything had improved. 'Not at all,' she told me. 'I feel that I'm being completely frozen out and now I'm unable to meet my billable hours.'

Anxious and unhappy, Hannah began to regularly feel sick before work. 'I can't eat breakfast these days,' she said, 'and I'm not sleeping. I know this is affecting all of my relationships. I feel like no one wants to be around me at the moment.' I knew from having witnessed the damage this kind of passive aggressive behaviour does with other clients that the best option for Hannah was to move on from the role – and ideally, quickly. But like other clients who had encountered the same thing, her confidence was at an all-time low and when I asked if she would consider leaving, Hannah told me that the thought of searching for a new role was just too overwhelming.

It was another six months and her work situation worsening before Hannah finally had the courage to resign. When she emailed me later that year, she wrote, 'I had no idea how bad it had become, Kate. I had become so used to the toxicity in that workplace that I didn't realise how sick it was making me. It is only now that I feel so respected, valued and *happy* again that I can see how destructive it was for my wellbeing as well as my confidence.'

If you think back to a time when you felt completely connected (to yourself, to others, to the life you were living), it's likely that you recall that you also felt totally at peace with yourself. Maybe you have experienced such a moment with a lover or friend, or in the company of a family member who accepts you just as you are. Some feel it when their dog greets them at the door with a tail and body that wags with joy. If you rarely feel this connection with other sentient beings, perhaps you have felt it when running, in a yoga class or witnessing music, art or nature that moved you so deeply that you connected with something bigger and more significant than yourself.

After two decades of working with clients, I have come to learn that when we feel connected to ourselves, there's an inner knowing, an inherent wisdom that signals to us that *we have our own answers within.* Each of us also has our own unique way of contributing to the world and if we can trust both of these things and act upon this wisdom, we're already on the pathway to confidence.

This recognition might begin as the smallest flicker, but when you set out to create and maintain this connection with yourself and you begin to listen to what your body is telling you, you'll also access a deeper connection with your intuition. Doing so will help to give you the courage to say with conviction, *'This is who I am, and there's room for me in this world.'* It's from this place you'll find the courage to take small steps in your chosen direction.

ELEVEN

Connect to your strengths

Almost universally, people seek out coaches, counsellors or therapists when they feel something is wrong with them, not when they discover something they do well. Given that our brains are wired to focus disproportionately on the negative, this focus on weaknesses over strengths isn't surprising, but it really works against us.

Taking a strengths-based approach to life doesn't mean ignoring or avoiding weaknesses – it simply means being aware of the things we do well and focusing on those while seeking to minimise the impact of our weaknesses. With this knowledge, we'll be able to craft lives that mostly engage our strengths. If this isn't possible, we can at least carve out extra time for tasks that call on weaknesses or ask for support from friends or colleagues for whom these are strengths.

Research into the success of taking a strengths-based approach in various contexts has shown over and over that using innate strengths helps us to feel energised and engaged at work. What's more, regularly engaging a top strength makes us more likely to move into a flow state, which in turn leads to a deeper sense of fulfilment in life. Further research shows a host of benefits for mental health and wellbeing, as well as self-confidence, when people engage more of their strengths in the workplace. According to Dr Michelle McQuaid, the many benefits of using more of your strengths at work include:

- Lower levels of depression, higher levels of vitality and good mental health.
- Higher levels of positivity and reduced stress. In particular, the character strengths of kindness, social intelligence, self-regulation and perspective appear to create a shield against the negative effects of stress and trauma.
- Feeling healthier and having more energy due to being more likely to pursue healthy behaviours and activities.
- Greater life satisfaction.
- Faster growth and development, especially when learning something new, difficult, or something you perceive to be difficult.
- Increased creativity and agility at work, since developing strengths helps to foster feelings of authenticity, vitality and concentration. This can make us better able to adapt to change and more inclined to participate in creative and proactive behaviours. It also makes us likely to pay attention to detail and work harder.
- Deriving greater satisfaction and meaning from work. People who use four or more of their top character strengths at work are more likely to experience greater job satisfaction, pleasure and meaning.

- Greater engagement in work: Employees who have opportunities to regularly use their strengths are up to six times more engaged in what they're doing.
- More confidence. Knowing your strengths and using them are two things that are both significantly associated with self-efficacy, self-esteem, self-acceptance and self-confidence.

Clearly, there are many upsides to using our strengths, but this doesn't stop most of us from believing that shoring up a weakness is the best way to improve ourselves, especially when it comes to our work. In a 2022 global workplace study, participants were asked the following question: *Which is more helpful for success: building on strengths or fixing weaknesses?* Less than 20 per cent of the participants answered 'building on strengths'. The overwhelming majority believed we needed to focus on improving our weaknesses. In fact, the exact opposite is true. Building on strengths is a faster and far more effective route to success than trying to improve on a weakness.

The best leaders in the world understand that *strengths* are the true areas for development; weaknesses simply become areas to manage around. These leaders know that they get the most growth, the most improvement on performance and the best return on their investment when they focus on maximising someone's strengths. When 80,000 managers were interviewed about their approach to management, the elite, top-performing managers in this group all had one thing in common: they viewed each of the members of their team as unique, and as having different abilities. The leaders' job was to define the role that each person played.

Marcus Buckingham, head of the research institute that conducted this global study, likens these managers to chess players. Once they've identified which pieces they have on their board, they don't waste time 'trying to turn their rook into a bishop'. Instead, they identify where each person has a competitive advantage, and then they figure out how to maximise their potential intelligently.

Rather than a person's weak areas becoming 'areas of opportunity' or 'areas for development', the goal is to help individuals excel by capitalising on their natural skills, not by making them a good 'all-rounder'.

Embrace the idea of growing your strengths

Why, then, do so many of us continue pouring energy into fixing our weaknesses or obsessing over our perceived flaws? Part of the answer lies in our natural tendency to focus on the negative, but another answer lies in the way we view our strengths and weaknesses. In research spanning six different studies, people were asked to describe a future version of themselves. The majority of participants expected that their current strengths would be the same in the future but their areas of weakness would have improved. They viewed their strengths as being constant and relatively fixed – what is often called a 'fixed mindset' (i.e., the belief that our strengths are set and cannot be improved on). Yet, for some reason, these same people viewed their weaknesses as being much more malleable. They believed it *would* be possible for those to be improved on because they displayed a 'growth mindset' towards their weaknesses. For this reason, they were *more* motivated to try and improve on a weakness than they were to invest time and energy into building on an existing strength.

The excellent news for all of us is that these assumptions are wrong. Strengths are much more malleable than we think. This applies equally to introverts, whose gifts are frequently overlooked by parents, managers or mentors hoping to turn introverted bishops into extroverted rooks.

Sadly, many of the introverts I work with skip over their strengths and berate themselves for things they perceive as weaknesses or shortcomings. Sandy is a brilliant and gentle yin yoga teacher, but she lacks the skill and the confidence to do mass marketing. Evan is an engineer with wonderful attention to detail but he's not great at workplace networking. Lucy, who is new in a leadership role, has excellent relationships with her team but she feels she could be more assertive.

Often, when we examine these weaknesses together, clients realise that these are simply extroverted ideals they've been struggling to live up to. When we explore the opposite of this ideal, they are often pleasantly surprised to find that their 'weakness' is masking a strength they didn't know they had.

Take the following headline, for example: 'Research shows that extroverts process information faster than introverts.' A sensitive introvert reading this sliver of information might infer that extroverts are more intelligent than introverts. However, if they read the article, they'll discover that this slower speed is a result of the fact that introverts tend to process information more *thoughtfully* than extroverts. Because of this, introverts tend to understand an idea better before they move on. Thinking more deeply isn't a weakness at all. It's a strength.

In Sandy's case, her teaching style, which connects so deeply with class participants, speaks for itself and marketing to the masses isn't something she's ever going to need – word of mouth means her classes are already full. Evan's exceptional work and his natural humility means his colleagues and manager like him and put him forward for great projects – he doesn't need to network to build workplace relationships. And Lucy's thoughtful interpersonal skills mean her team respect her already. She might benefit from getting more comfortable with open communication in a difficult moment, but she doesn't need to be overly focused on being assertive.

Flip the script on a weakness

Write down something you consider an area of weakness for you, then spend some time considering whether this is a true weakness, or simply an extroverted ideal that you've been struggling to meet. Could turning this weakness on its head reveal a strength? It did for Mary.

Mary works in the creative department of an ad agency with a lot of big personalities. During meetings, she takes notes while her co-workers brainstorm ideas for taglines, slogans and pitch concepts. Though she is expected to contribute, too, Mary finds coming up with ideas on the spot hard, especially when everyone else is throwing out their ideas. Since starting work at the agency, she has come to see this as a major career weakness.

By examining this perceived weakness together, Mary was able to see her behaviour for what it was: a way her creative process differs from that of her extroverted colleagues. 'I always contribute ideas,' she said. 'I just do it by email later rather than in the room because

I need to be able to think quietly before I know what I want to say.' Many of Mary's ideas and concepts have been used in projects, so this way of working is obviously successful, not only for her but also for the team. Her ability to listen and think deeply is a great asset, not a weakness.

Identify your natural strengths

We already know that Western culture reserves most of its praise for the shiny strengths of extroverts. You're likely reading this book because you've expended a lot of your own energy worrying about the fact that you don't have these strengths. My guess is that you've tried to cultivate several of them. In a moment, I'll show you how to identify your unique stable of strengths, but first I want to shine a light on the many strengths associated with being an introvert. They may not be as shouted about as extrovert strengths, but increasingly, the world is catching on to the fact that they are equally valuable and every bit as powerful. In many cases, they are even outright advantages.

An article on the website *Introvert, Dear,* points to seven key advantages that introverts have over extroverts.

1. **Introverts make low-maintenance friends and colleagues.** This is a real asset in many contexts since introverts respect the space of others and are very unlikely to ever be described as obnoxious, needy or disruptive.

2. **Introverts have creative, original minds.** Introverts tend to be less influenced by what is trending, so they follow their own preferences, often gravitating to things that others may see as niche or obscure.

3. **Introverts are shrewd decision-makers and are good at solving problems.** Because they are wired to be more cautious and to deliberate thoughtfully before reaching a decision, introverts think things through carefully and often make more calculated decisions – often on their own. Their inclination to take time to be alone means they spend more time reflecting and observing. This helps them gather information and makes them a good judge of character, among other things.

4. **Introverts are excellent listeners.** They are more likely to focus intently on what another person is trying to express than extroverts. This makes it easy for people to confide in them. And because they are often private by nature, they understand that it can be difficult to open up to and trust other people, and are therefore likely to work harder to be trustworthy themselves.

5. **Introverts are good at focusing deeply and blocking out distractions.** They give less attention to socialising than extroverts and can dive deeply into research or writing for long periods of time. This ability can make it easier for them to become experts in their field.

6. **They have the ability to cultivate deep relationships.** We'll explore this point more in chapter 14 because connecting with others is something I view as one of our greatest strengths. It's true that introverts have less social energy than extroverts, but, usually, this makes us more selective about who we spend our time with. For the introvert, it's quality over quantity that counts. Because of this we nurture and cherish our relationships.

7. **Introverts are independent and tend to require less supervision.** In the context of the working world, especially, this can give us a major advantage over our extroverted peers. Typically, we require fewer 'check-ins' with managers, as they are able to trust that we can do our job without being distracted or socialising the way a more extroverted person who describes themselves as 'a team player' might.

The gifts of being a highly sensitive person (HSP)

Many of the introverts who come to see me also happen to be highly sensitive people (HSPs) who share characteristics such as being easily overwhelmed by crowds, loud noises or violence on television. They often feel that they've been labelled as overly emotional, and their sensitive nature has marked them as different since childhood. Consequently, many HSPs feel that there's something wrong with them, but according to Dr Elaine Aron, a psychologist who's been researching HSPs for more than 30 years, this simply isn't the case. Being highly sensitive is an innate personality trait biologists have found in over 100 species. It affects between 15 and 20 per cent of the population and often overlaps with being an introvert. Just like introversion, being an HSP comes with its own set of extraordinary gifts. A few of these are listed below.

1. **Being extremely empathetic.** You feel things deeply, and this means you can build strong relationships that contribute to making you happier and more fulfilled.

2. **Having great observation skills.** You notice even slight changes in your environment and in other people. You can pick up on cues that others miss.

3. **Having a good nose for danger.** Being able to pick up on tiny changes around you makes it easier for you to identify danger and avoid unnecessary conflicts better than most other people.

4. **Having fantastic social skills.** Thanks to your ability to 'read people', you work well in teams, can boost positivity and are excellent at noticing when another person is in need of something – whether that's space, comfort or support.

5. **Being gentle and kind.** Not only are you great at picking up on signals other people send, but you are also likely to be the type of person who does something to help.

6. **Having a strong sense of intuition.** Often, you may not be able to explain how you know the things you know, but you trust this intuition to guide you. It can often simplify the decision-making process.

7. **Likely to see the good in everything.** HSPs tend to be appreciative and humble, so you might be great at letting those you care about know that they are valued. This often means that friends, work colleagues and employers view you very positively. Seeing good in everything (though this doesn't always extend to yourself) can help you stay positive and motivated.

If you're an HSP, it's likely that you'll have several of these qualities, but each sensitive person is different. Free online assessments such as the one specifically for HSPs on the Highly Sensitive Person website can help you pinpoint your specific strengths. Some may be known to you already while others might come as a pleasant surprise.

Identify your core strengths

Because we live with them every day, most of us are blind to our own strengths. We might not even see them as strengths because we assume they are qualities everyone else possesses, too. As introverts, we are also more inclined to downplay a strength than we are to honour it, and this is detrimental to our sense of worth as well as our confidence.

When we acknowledge and lean into our innate strengths, we start to believe in our inherent value and trust in our infinite worth. By embracing our uniqueness and exploring the ways we can use our natural strengths more every day, our lives become richer and more meaningful.

My three favourite tools for uncovering your strengths

Though there are many methods for discovering your strengths, these are my personal favourites, and the ones I use with my clients.

1. Alex Linley's Strengthspotting Tips
2. VIA (Values In Action) Signature Strengths Survey
3. Cappfinity Strengths Profile

1. Alex Linley's Strengthspotting Tips

Before you complete the other profiling tools, I recommend journalling your responses to the following questions, which I've adapted from Alex Linley's book *Average To A+*.

1. Which childhood activities do you still love and feel energised by?
2. When do you feel most like your true self?

3. Which activities or skills come most naturally to you?
4. What skills or strengths are you complimented about?
5. Where do you learn most quickly?
6. When do you find yourself naturally motivated?

2. VIA Signature Strengths Survey

On the VIA Signature Strengths website, you'll find a free survey – the results of which can be viewed online. It takes around 15 minutes to complete, and the results rank all 24 of the strengths. Your 'signature strengths' are the top-ranked strengths, and these are also the characteristics that best describe the positive aspects of your personality.

3. Cappfinity Strengths Profile

The free assessment at strengthsprofile.com takes around 15 minutes to complete and reveals your top three strengths, three unrealised strengths, two learned behaviours and one weakness. Many clients opt to upgrade to the paid Introductory profile which expands on the results above and most find that this test helps them in the workplace.

Explore your shadow strengths

Author Sally Kempton writes about another concept I love: finding our 'positive shadow'. Unlike the shadow self (which we'll explore more in the next chapter), the positive shadow represents the 'unowned golden qualities' in us. We can shine a light on this golden part of ourselves in the same way we search for our shadow self: by noticing when we are projecting it on to others. The next time you find yourself admiring or idealising another person, reflect on what it is specifically about them that elicits this feeling in you. By looking deeper, you can start to question whether the qualities you are seeing in them mirror qualities hidden inside you. Kempton recommends that we also search for clues to our own 'unexpressed or uncultivated strengths' in the people we've fallen in love with, our closest friends, and those we idolised in our youth.

Rediscovering Sally's description of embracing 'unowned golden qualities' was timely and wonderful for me. I have long admired (and as much as I'd prefer not to admit it, felt somewhat envious of) people who are comfortable to market themselves and sell their services effortlessly. Like my yoga teacher client, Sandy, marketing doesn't come naturally to me. I have always felt uncomfortable putting myself out there but a story a colleague shared recently changed the way I view this.

'Imagine a city where there were no health services at all,' she suggested. 'No doctors, no hospitals, no pharmacies. And imagine you had just trained in medicine and opened a wonderful little clinic, but your introversion made you want to stay hidden. How will people who need your services know your clinic exists?'

I love how this story flips the idea of marketing on its head. Each of us has a unique set of gifts to share and if we hide those gifts from the world, there's no way we can make our contribution and no opportunity to embrace true meaning. Instead of thinking of marketing as selling, we can think of it as service.

In the months since hearing this story, I'm working on baby steps to be more comfortable with marketing. As my daughter Meg reminded me, 'Just like you once feared public speaking, take the small steps and let yourself do it like a beginner for now. One day, it will be more effortless and you might even find you enjoy it.'

Expand your definition of a strength

When I received the results of my own VIA Strength Survey many years ago, the strength ranked in my number-one spot left me feeling confused. It wasn't 'social intelligence' or 'fairness', which I'd assumed it would be, but rather, 'appreciation of beauty' – not something I considered a strength, let alone powerful or even unique.

However, as I sat with this new piece of information, I began to see all the ways that appreciating beauty *was*, in fact, very true of me. I've always drawn energy and joy from being in nature, and appreciation of beauty is a big reason for this. Since childhood, I've noticed small things that others seem to miss: the subtle changes of light in the seasons, the smell of the eucalypts after the rain, the magnificence of a single flower, the texture of shells and rocks on a beach. The more I reflected, the more I came to realise that these small life moments have not only filled me with joy since childhood, they have been the moments that have brought my awareness fully into the present moment and made me feel most alive.

This strength touches almost every aspect of my life, making our everyday lives more beautiful. It drives my ongoing love of cooking and baking, it gives me the energy to keep working on our garden and it's the energising force that gets me out of bed early every morning to walk through our local bush reserve.

It also shapes my work in many ways. I look for and find the beauty in every client I work with and spend many hours choosing images for my website and presentations to ensure they are visually appealing.

If your top strengths initially strike you as 'soft strengths', I encourage you to challenge how you define them. When embraced and used intelligently, strengths such as 'modesty', 'hope' or 'kindness' can wield immense power and influence.

Embracing 'soft strengths': Tom's story

My client Tom found a way to do this. A gentle, thoughtful man who worked as a senior policy officer in a state government department, Tom told me about a recent performance appraisal. For the first time in five years, he had a female manager, Ellie, and he was surprised when she called out his 'soft strengths'.

She praised his willingness to support younger team members when he was already busy and acknowledged his ongoing efforts to encourage the team to put in their best work on their current project. Despite a growing sense of apathy and frustration in the office after a recent change in government, Tom told his colleagues, 'I know it feels disheartening, but I think we can get this policy implemented. If we make it robust, we still have a good chance of selling it to the new minister.'

His compassion and patience when others might have expressed frustration was visible to Ellie, and his ongoing encouragement of other team members signalled his ability to hold on to hope when others gave up more easily.

The surprising master strength

When Martin Seligman and 24 other researchers gathered to discuss which strengths to include on the VIA list of core strengths, 'love' was very high on everyone's list. Initially, the group defined this strength as a person's 'capacity TO love'; however, one of the group, George Vaillant, chastised them for ignoring the capacity to BE loved by another person.

Vaillant's opinion counted for a lot since he was the head of the landmark Grant Study (often referred to as the 'Harvard Study') – an ongoing study of Harvard alumni that tracked the developmental trajectories of Harvard graduates. At the time of this gathering, the Grant Study had been running for nearly 70 years, and through this work, Vaillant and his colleagues had discovered that the capacity to love *and* be loved was the strength most clearly linked to a person's wellbeing at the age of 80.

This master strength was an important revelation, and a reminder of how important self-worth is to this equation because a person must first feel that they are *worthy* of love in order to *allow* themselves to be loved. They must also be courageous enough to let themselves be known and seen by others for who they really are. This is such a crucial aspect of quiet confidence because so many introverts stay hidden.

Strengthen your strengths

Now that you've identified your strengths, it's time to get strategic about how to use them so you can identify ways of developing them further. I encourage you to use a journal for this exercise so that you can revisit what you've written and add new ideas as they occur to you. You might also note which strategies worked well, and which didn't.

When brainstorming these ideas, apply a kaizen-like approach of 'small steps'. Change doesn't need to be big or dramatic to be effective and in fact, it's the small, simple changes that can be implemented immediately and easily repeated that usually yield the most impressive results.

1. Review your strengths above and write a paragraph or two about how you currently use these strengths at work and in your personal life.

2. If you discover one or two strengths that you're not engaging very often, brainstorm a few ways you can bring these strengths to life. For example, if you identify the strength of 'humour' but recognise you're not being as light as you once were, consider a few ways to laugh more. Watch a comedy series, share funny memes with a friend or try recalling amusing stories from your childhood.

3. If you realise that you overuse a particular strength (which can actually be draining), make a note of how you can downplay it. For example, if you, like many introverts, have a strength of 'kindness and compassion', take note of where you instantly agree to giving up your time for other people. Dialling these strengths down might be easier if you establish the regular habit of self-care, such as setting aside Sunday afternoons for resting or joining a couple of weekly meditation classes.

4. Looking at your top strengths, ask yourself whether any of these criteria apply:

   - Do you feel a sense of ownership of the strength? (I.e., does it feel like the 'real you'?)
   - Can you identify any new ways to engage this strength?
   - Do you feel invigorated (rather than exhausted) while using this strength? If your answer is exhausted, it's likely you're overusing it.
   - Do you have personal projects that utilise this strength?

5. Look back at the strengths that didn't make it to the top of your list. Some may be attributes you simply don't enjoy using, but there's a chance that one or two are 'unrealised strengths', or in other words, qualities you have in areas where you're not allowing yourself to shine. Make a note of how you can use these more often. There may be others you consider to be weaknesses. Can you avoid using these altogether by outsourcing tasks or delegating? Are there others that you need to build in order to feel more fulfilled or energised? Are there some you can simply let go of?

Connect with your goals

In Part One: Meaning, we spoke about setting goals that align with your values. Now I'll share how you can marry the strengths you've just uncovered with those goals, as well as bringing in some ideas about 'meaning'. These simple steps can boost your ability to achieve a goal, because using skills and talents that come naturally to you *and* thinking about how your goals make a difference to other people, makes doing hard things easier and more enjoyable. In contrast, trying to meet a goal by pressuring yourself into doing things you're not good at, or being someone you are not, is deflating and, ultimately, confidence-destroying.

Using your strengths as often as possible is a sure way to foster trust in your own capabilities. In the magical space where meaning and strengths collide, achieving goals is often a by-product of doing something that energises and inspires us.

1. On one piece of paper, write down the value-aligned goals you set for yourself.
2. On a second piece of paper, make a list of your top five strengths.

3. Working through each goal, brainstorm ways to use two or more of these strengths to aid your progress. If necessary, break each goal into smaller steps, as this might help you identify which strengths are best suited to achieving certain steps. As always, apply a kaizen-like approach by thinking of small, consistent actions rather than grand, sweeping ones. Write down all of these ideas, being as specific as possible about the actions you will take.

4. Next, review the strengths that didn't make your top five. Could any of these be applied to achieving your goals? Again, write down your ideas and be specific about the actions.

5. Choose one goal to focus on for the next week and circle one of the ideas you had for achieving it. Commit to implementing this small action every day for the next seven days.

6. As you focus on this goal, also think about how achieving it might benefit other people. For example, the goal of committing to daily exercise might improve your mood for your partner or make you more positive around your colleagues. The goal of setting up a savings plan might mean you can help your kids out with their university fees or give your parents a hand as they're ageing.

7. Revisit this brainstorming exercise at the end of the week and evaluate how successful you've been at using your strengths and meaning to pursue your goals. If something you're doing isn't working, ask yourself why. Perhaps you've chosen goals that don't align with your true values and strengths?

TWELVE

(Re)connect to your confident self

Many people are sceptical when I tell them that they already have a confident part of their personality, perhaps because they see confidence as something that needs to be constructed from the ground up rather than something that is innate within all of us. But no matter how uncertain you might feel, the foundation of confidence really does exist within you – it may just be hidden right now. Uncovering it is well worth the work because your 'confident self' is an ally and ultimately, it can become your greatest strength.

If we separate the word 'confidence' from the contemporary idea of it and define it as originally intended – as *trust in oneself* – it becomes clear why connecting to yourself and knowing yourself better are so vital to building confidence.

Even so, my clients sometimes come to me with briefs that are less about making this connection and more about how they can change in order to fit in. Many of these creative, intelligent and sensitive people have received messages that they're wrong in some way – maybe they aren't vocal enough, quick enough or tough enough for this busy world – and that's what they want to address.

Instead, I try to help them see that they're not defective at all. They are valuable, worthy and full of gifts that can be put to use right away. I try to guide people back to the quietly confident part of themselves they've lost touch with. I found my way back to this part of myself through years of meditation, and others find it in unexpected places – during a life transition, as the result of an impactful experience, or in a moment of strong emotion. They might even experience some kind of epiphany, like the one Elizabeth (Liz) Gilbert describes in the first scene of her autobiographical novel *Eat, Pray, Love*.

The book opens with Liz on the floor of her bathroom in the middle of the night. Her messy divorce has drained her confidence and left her feeling despondent and near suicidal. Suddenly, in the dark, she hears an unfamiliar but very kind, patient voice say, 'Go back to bed, Liz.' Which she does.

Decades after writing this scene, Liz explained that the voice she heard that night was different from anything she'd heard before. She hadn't grown up listening to the sort of kindness or tenderness she heard in this voice, and she was drawn to it. In the days that followed that late-night epiphany, she says she 'developed a relationship with this voice' and began writing to herself from its point of view to 'soothe her in her despair'. For more than 20 years, she has kept up the practice of writing to herself from this unconditionally loving voice. She even credits it with getting her through bouts of depression, anxiety, crisis and despondency, and for teaching her to speak to the more fearful parts of herself.

This voice is what I would call her wise, knowing, confident self. By recognising it as a powerful supporter and keeping the lines of communication open through her daily writing practice, Liz has been able to access this part of herself easily and use it to soothe the more fragile aspects of her nature.

Glennon Doyle's experience was similar when she connected to the 'Knowing'. Sinking into a pile of clothes in her closet, she challenged herself to meditate for ten minutes each day, and through this practice discovered a place she'd never known existed: somewhere with no voices and no panic.

I think of this aspect as our 'inner light', and my own awareness of it mirrors the experiences of these two women. Learning meditation many years ago gave me access to a deep sense of inner stillness, which I find hugely helpful during challenging moments. Sometime later, while doing my teacher training in self-compassion, I learned that each of us also has a kind and caring aspect of ourselves that can soothe our difficult emotions. And later again, I came across American psychiatrist Dr Richard C. Schwartz's work on Internal Family Systems (IFS), an approach I found profoundly enlightening.

This innately confident aspect of ourselves is what Dr Schwartz calls 'Self' energy and this aspect exists within each of us. It's a part of ourselves that has its own innate wisdom and regardless of our life experiences, doesn't need to grow or change or develop – it is infinitely valuable as it is. (I explore in depth Dr Schwartz's IFS approach and the 'Self' on pages 155–8.)

This concept of the 'Self' as a wise, knowing inner wisdom became the bridge that brought the two elements of stillness and compassionate wisdom together for me. Through this, I've also been able to cultivate a much stronger connection with my intuition, which is something the wise, confident self relies on for guidance.

Intuition

Unlike conscious reasoning, which happens in the brain, intuition is thought to be felt or sensed in the body. It's something that we all experience, and there are different layers to it.

1. **Gut instinct:** This is the most primal form of intuition – our animal nature encouraging us to pursue something for our survival (a romantic interest, perhaps), or alerting us to danger when we sense changes in our environment on a subconscious level. It typically shows up as a 'feeling' when you meet a new person or walk into an unfamiliar place, and the messages it sends are binary: Yes/No. Stop/Run.

   Many people report that this sensation comes from their belly area (hence the term 'gut instinct'), and there's an excellent reason for this: the enteric nervous system located in our gut is lined with 100 million nerve cells that are constantly sending messages to the brain. Though the jury is still out on exactly how this system impacts our thoughts, we do know for certain that things we experience in our bodies impact our brains.

2. **Emotional intuition:** The second layer of intuition is more connected to our heart. It's a subconscious social awareness that picks up on the subtle physical signals that others are sending. This is the type of intuition that tells you whether compassion is called for, whether someone needs help or whether it would be best not to tell that person the secret

that's on the tip of your tongue. This type of wisdom is also connected to our true feelings and desires and it's the best source of information when we are unsure of what it is that we want.

How to tune in to your intuition

When we're being intuitive, we're not actively thinking or analysing; we're turning our awareness within and accessing information deep inside us. Once you connect with intuition, you'll likely get better at noticing these fleeting insights coming from within. The next part of the puzzle is learning how to listen to your intuition and use it to guide the confident part of yourself.

Meditation

Since intuition often alerts us to danger, it can sometimes be difficult to tell the difference between intuition and self-doubt, anxiety or fear. This is why it's easiest to connect with genuine intuition when we're in a state of calm. For this reason, a regular meditation practice is the most effective way to cultivate the kind of self-awareness that helps us connect with intuition. As little as ten minutes of quiet reflection at the beginning of each day can help build awareness of this inner wisdom. If you're new to meditation, I suggest beginning with guided meditations. The Insight Timer meditation app is one of my favourites. It's free and there are hundreds of meditations to choose from, including several of mine. One in particular will help with this – it's called 'Connect with Your Inner Wisdom'.

Regardless of whether you meditate or not, spend an hour or two each week in stillness, without any distractions or entertainment. If possible, get into nature, which will help lower your cortisol levels and help you feel grounded. Walking and running are sometimes referred to as 'moving meditation' and they're also effective because rhythmic movement and physical relaxation make it easier to tune in to our intuition.

Most commonly, however, the problem isn't that we can't access our intuition, it's that we don't listen to it. We feel those little niggles, but if they're telling us things we'd rather not hear, we might direct our attention elsewhere.

Trust your gut instinct: Kat's story

My client Kat was seeing me for career coaching but when we started to speak about her overall sense of fulfilment, she confessed that her relationship with her partner seemed to be undermining her self-esteem.

Kat and Ritchie had been together for a couple of years when she started sensing something wasn't quite right. While away on a work trip, she called Ritchie one evening and he stepped away from his 'group of colleagues' to speak with her. She noticed his voice was different as they chatted, and he was reluctant to share any details about who he was with and where.

Later, when Kat was back at home, she raised her concerns with Ritchie. He admitted he'd been out with a female colleague but insisted they were only friends.

Over the ensuing months, there were other small signs of dishonesty. Money going missing from their shared bank account, an unexplained credit card charge and surreptitious bouts of late-night texting. Kat told me she'd been ignoring these things because she didn't want to face the consequences of listening to what her instincts were now screaming.

Her fears were realised when she read some messages on his mobile. After trusting her gut instinct, Kat eventually left the relationship. She didn't want to spend her life looking over her shoulder, and she valued herself enough to believe she'd meet someone who would treat her more respectfully.

Try to keep listening rather than ignoring your gut instinct or rationalising your way out of the messages it sends you. Be curious about the wisdom it is offering.

Dream journals

Another way to access intuition is to let your subconscious guide you while you're asleep. Spend a couple of weeks paying attention to your dreams. Keep a notebook beside your bed and upon waking, jot down whatever elements of your dream you remember. Even just a sentence or two is a good start. Recall how you were feeling in your dream and think about how those feelings show up in your everyday life. Consider also that the characters in your dreams might represent different aspects of yourself.

While it's tempting to look to a dream analyst to decipher your dreams, trust your instincts about your own interpretations. You know yourself better than anyone, and with an open and curious mind, it's likely you'll learn to interpret the messages on your own.

You might also want to try tapping in to the transition between wakefulness and sleep. Sometimes our sleepy subconscious mind can guide us in ways we're less open to when we're using our rational, waking mind. This brief transition between wakefulness and sleep (a state known as hypnagogia) is a time when we often find a moment of clarity or discover the answer to a problem that feels inherently right.

Where have you displayed confidence in the past?

One of the reasons many of us lose touch with our confidence is that we don't slow down to acknowledge the things we've already achieved.

Revisiting your strengths: Julia's story

I helped Julia to do this during a time she felt very low in confidence. A new mum with a ten-month-old son, Julia was worried about returning to work. 'I love motherhood,' she said, 'but no one tells you how lonely and boring it can be. I feel incredibly isolated and I've completely lost my confidence. I don't even know what I have to offer anymore.'

As well as the long days spent on her own with her baby boy, on the few occasions Julia and her husband Sam had attended social events, she found people turning away from her in conversation. 'I've never felt less like I matter,' she reflected, 'and it has really stripped away my confidence.'

I invited Julia to tell me a little about her life pre-baby and her face was instantly illuminated. 'Oh, I was happy and funny and courageous,' she laughed. 'I loved my job and I had such great relationships with my little team. I felt like I was able to be the best version of myself. These days I can't even find that part of me. I feel so serious and drained by the end of the day, that I know I'm not great company for Sam.'

Julia shared a few stories about her working life before the baby and how much she had enjoyed her role as a senior publicist in a small PR agency. 'It was a role that really played to my strengths. There was always a lovely light banter in the office and I felt that I was good at mentoring my young team. Although it was pretty high pressure at times, everyone was thriving.'

Since becoming a mother, Julia had lost touch with her workmates as well as the qualities that made her feel like the best version of herself. Our brief conversation sparked enough memory for her to recognise that going back into the office part-time might be the best thing for her, her marriage and ultimately even her baby.

Writing a list of all the things you've accomplished or chatting about them with a friend can be a great way of reminding yourself of the many different ways you have already demonstrated confidence and competence in your life. Next to each achievement, jot down the role confidence played. For example, if moving to a new country was on your list, remind yourself that took courage and curiosity to make that decision.

Resist the urge to *only* focus on the big achievements on society's checklist: education, house, car, job, partner, children, etc. By all means include them, but also think smaller. This past year alone, you've probably shown confidence many more times than you realise. Scroll back through photographs to remind you of things you're forgetting. The weekend away you saved up for, the night you opened up to a friend, or the job interview you had to take an aptitude test for.

Next, review your calendar, because there are bound to be appointments that jog your memory: work meetings you were nervous about, tough projects that turned out well, a dentist appointment you endured, or a new friend you invited for coffee. Once you finish this 'year in review', keep the list somewhere visible and look at it whenever you need a reminder that you can be confident because you *already* possess confidence.

THIRTEEN

Connect to your other 'selves' (all of them)

Do I contradict myself?
Very well then I contradict myself,
(I am large, I contain multitudes).

When American poet Walt Whitman wrote this in 1850, it was risky for a person to admit that they 'contained multitudes'. This marked them as odd at best, or mentally ill at worst. For centuries, the dominant theory about the human mind was that it was a singular *mono-mind* that each of us needed to control and manage. Mainstream religions also supported this theory, and instructed followers to tame their 'monkey mind' (Buddhism) and suppress their sinful urges (Christianity). Contradictory voices needed to be eliminated because they didn't represent the true self.

The mono-mind theory made sense on paper, but it didn't *feel* true for anyone who'd ever had the experience of arguing with . . . themselves. The subversive idea that the mind is naturally multiple (and healthily so) continued to pop up again and again throughout Western culture and some Eastern cultures, but it was shut down and pathologised in favour of the mono-mind. Still, people found ways to describe the conflict these multiple selves were causing within them. Expressions like 'fighting fear', 'resisting temptation', 'battling anger' and 'quieting rage' became commonplace. A person who failed to reach a goal might blame 'self-sabotage', and it was widely acknowledged that we are often 'our own worst enemy'. In moments of indecision, who hasn't felt conflicted? 'A part of me wants this, but another part wants that.' The language we use to talk about our inner world is at times combative and contradictory.

Like so many others, Whitman recognised that his mind – or whatever it was that made him *him* – was not a singular thing with a singular point of view, but rather several *parts* vying for control and contradicting each other in the process. He didn't need a psychiatrist to confirm this because he knew it intuitively.

In the 1980s, more than a century after Whitman had written about his 'multitudes', Dr Richard C. Schwartz found evidence that we are all 'naturally multiple', and that this was actually a good thing. At the beginning of his career, Schwartz had also subscribed to the mono-mind theory. However, when patients at his family clinic sought help with destructive urges such as bingeing and purging, and he coached them to suppress those urges, he had little success. If anything, this approach made his patients lean into their destructive behaviours even more, and even made these urges stronger.

As a family therapist, Schwartz had been trained to see families as individual systems operating in very specific contexts. They were delicate ecosystems. A small change in one area had the power to affect all the others. An argument between a mother and daughter might cause a father to withdraw or other siblings to act out, for example.

The inner worlds his patients revealed echoed a dynamic Schwartz knew well: that of a family. He came to believe that what we generally call *thinking* might also be considered an internal family made up of many sub-minds that are constantly interacting inside of us. And just like a family, these 'personalities', 'selves', 'parts' or 'aspects' (I'll use these terms interchangeably throughout the book) each have their own preferences and resources.

Schwartz decided to approach the destructive urges he saw in his clients the same way he'd approach a difficult family member. He encouraged his patients to tune in to the sensations they were feeling and turn towards those difficult experiences. He asked them to listen to the thoughts occupying their minds, and then express those views out loud. Patient after patient detailed the things their critical voices were saying. They also explained how much pain those thoughts caused them, and how that pain often compelled them to do something destructive that they later felt shame over.

By working *with* instead of against these critical voices, something remarkable happened: his patients finally began to heal. This led Schwartz to the realisation that even our most destructive parts have positive intentions. If we can appreciate this and show compassion to *all* of the parts of ourselves, we can change our internal experience.

Based on this work, Schwartz created the therapeutic approach known as Internal Family Systems (IFS), which recognises three key parts, which I have simplified here:

1. Vulnerable Selves (the disowned and most sensitive parts of us)
2. Protectors
3. The Self

Meet the selves

Because each of our parts is distinct and has its own goals, IFS teaches that the most effective way to heal and resolve inner conflict is to address each one directly. The goal of IFS isn't to eliminate the difficult parts or even to 'merge' all of the parts into one cohesive whole; it's simply to bring awareness to each part and then welcome it into the family.

1. The vulnerable selves

Each of us is born curious, sensitive, creative and playful. These aspects of our personality are innate, but the inevitable experiences of life can quickly quash our innocent trust and suppress these joyful aspects of ourselves. As we experience misunderstanding, neglect or rejection, our 'inner children' become more vulnerable.

These vulnerable selves start to believe negative things about themselves or the world (e.g., *I'm worthless and nobody cares about me*) and these beliefs shape our behaviour.

When we experience uncomfortable feelings such as fear, shame or low confidence, that's a sure sign that one (or more) of our vulnerable parts has been activated.

2. The protective selves

To prevent our inner children from being ridiculed or feeling pain, we quickly develop other aspects of ourselves to serve as their protectors. Their sole purpose is to protect our vulnerable children from the difficult emotions that accompany judgement, criticism, rejection or failure.

The protective parts vary in each of us, but generally, they include personalities with a common goal of controlling us or keeping us safe. Some of these might speak with mean or critical voices (like a strict parent or teacher), while others might adopt a people-pleasing approach, urging us to stay quiet and keep the peace, usually to help us stay connected to others. Some might even be perfectionists or intellectual analysts that keep us stuck in our heads – overthinking and overanalysing rather than taking action they deem to be too risky.

Since the stakes are so high, these protective selves often show up in the body as tightness or tension in the muscles, or restriction in your breathing. And although they mean well, the impact they can have on our life can be 'deadening', since they don't just stop us from feeling pain, they also stop us from experiencing joy.

3. The Self

Unlike our other selves, 'Self' energy isn't formed in response to trauma or experience. It is an innate force that is within all of us that can't be hurt and doesn't need to grow. It doesn't engage in arguments over which course of action to pursue or who gets to drive; it stands back and observes. In essence, it's the adult in the room. Rebecca Ray, author of *Setting Boundaries*, calls this part the Inner Leader, which I love because it calls to mind someone who is decisive, courageous and who takes action. 'Self' is also what I consider to be 'the confident self' – the wise part that exists within all of us that has faith in our own abilities.

When we connect with this aspect of ourselves, we connect to our sense of 'infinite worth' and our unique, singular light. We make contact with this energy most effectively when we invite the other aspects of our self to relax and open up space inside of us (this is most easily done during one of Schwartz's guided meditations, which are available on the Insight Timer app and also in his audiobook, *Greater Than the Sum of Our Parts*). Once accessed, some people experience this Self energy as a tingling energy in their fingers and toes (this is what is also known as the 'life force' of *chi* or *prana* in other disciplines). By creating a sense of spaciousness inside, we can access a place of wellbeing and 'enoughness'. As Dr Schwartz witnessed this Self emerging in different clients, he catalogued a list of its qualities that were common to almost everyone who experienced it. These became known as 'the eight C's':

Curiosity

Calm

Confidence

Compassion

Creativity

Clarity

Courage

Connectedness

The shadow self

Though the 'shadow self' doesn't play a role within the IFS framework, like a lot of the protectors, it's also reactive. Carl Jung coined the term 'shadow self' to describe the parts of us that we don't want to acknowledge – or, as he put it, 'the person you'd rather not be'. His use of the word 'shadow' was a nod to the yogic scriptures that influenced his work.

Our shadow self (or selves) is usually made up of our most immature parts. It's rooted in a primal part of ourselves, and often we are so scared by or ashamed of this side of ourselves that we push it away. Rather than face these negative qualities, our instinct is to hide or get rid of them so we can only show our 'good selves' to the world.

Facing your shadow: Audrey's story

Audrey, like Julia, is a relatively new mother, with an 18-month-old baby girl named Esther. Since having her daughter, Audrey has also been on parental leave and has found the experience of parenting confronting for different reasons to Julia. Audrey was beating herself up over how little she seems to achieve in a day.

'I could do so much more,' Audrey blurts out. 'I'm just secretly lazy.'

'How do you feel now that you've shared this with me?' I ask.

'Ashamed,' she replies. 'Like a failure.'

Audrey *isn't* a failure, though. Far from it. She's a normal person giving in to bouts of rest, the way many of us do – especially when raising infants. However, it's clear that her feelings of shame about *not always being productive* run deep.

Her admission of laziness is especially interesting given it's one of the qualities she most loathes in other people. In previous sessions, we've discussed how her husband Mark's occasional laziness is a huge trigger for her. She hates it when he doesn't make the bed, pick up his clothes or put away his dishes. Tellingly, Audrey feels a surge of anger when Mark watches television with Esther in the room, even though she admitted to me that she's done the same thing.

I suspected Audrey was struggling with Mark and herself because she was coming up against her 'shadow self'. It's suggested that when we resent someone or are triggered by a particular behaviour or quality in them, it's often because they are reflecting a negative aspect of ourselves back to us – one we'd rather not see. If we aren't aware of these shadow selves, they have the power to make us act out in unpredictable ways without understanding why. We might fly off the handle over something minor, or despair when we make a small mistake.

Interestingly, our shadow selves are usually the opposites of our conscious personality. This is certainly true of Audrey. From what I know of her, she prides herself on being an ambitious and together woman who can 'do it all'. That go-getting side of Audrey is what Jungian psychologists would call her 'Persona' (from the Latin word for mask). Behind it is where her authentic self and shadow self hide.

When we acknowledge a shadow quality and bring it into the light, it becomes possible for us to truly mature. Identifying shadow selves can be painful and uncomfortable because the parts we feel most ashamed of often have roots in our early childhood. Parents or teachers might have told us we were too sensitive, selfish, moody or angry, leading us to suppress or hide these qualities.

Showing compassion to yourself is essential because all of us have a shadow – you're not the only person who harbours feelings such as envy, guilt or greed. The process of bringing awareness to these less-desirable parts of our personality in order to better understand how they drive our behaviour and emotions is called 'shadow work', and it is an incredibly valuable tool in the pathway to healing. It requires a lot of patience and a lot of compassion, but the good news is that as you widen your understanding of your shadow, you'll also become more aware of your light.

Bring your shadow selves into the light

The following five prompts are based on spiritual teacher Sally Kempton's suggestions for beginning the process of bringing non-judgemental awareness to your shadow selves. These exercises might be uncomfortable initially, but the more you examine the shadow aspects of yourself, the less power they have over you.

1. What do others see in you?

Think about the traits that other people tend to criticise you for. What type of feedback do you get from bosses or co-workers? Do your family members complain that you are too bossy or hot-headed? Have friends mentioned that you can be a little flirtatious with other people's significant others? Look for common themes in these critiques, as these can be important clues to your shadow qualities. It's likely you won't feel great about what you hear, but if you can begin to be open and admit these flaws to yourself – and deal with the accompanying feelings of shame and embarrassment – you can begin to face the truth of who you are and be kinder to yourself about your imperfection.

2. What small irritations really burn you up?

Think about encounters with other people that leave you emotionally charged. These can be little things that shouldn't bother you but really do. For example, if slow-moving traffic drives you crazy, perhaps your anger comes from an entitled self who believes that life should be easy for you. If you bristle when a friend tells you about their recent win at work, dig into that. Do you feel threatened by their success because you've been procrastinating on your own project? As you look more closely at your hidden shadow feelings, they will begin to make more sense and eventually, they'll also lose their power over you.

3. Who can't you stand to be around?

Sometimes, for reasons we can't even explain, we can't stand a certain person. So much so that the very idea of being around them makes our skin crawl. Think back to being with someone who rubbed you the wrong way. Replay the interaction and try to put your finger on the thing that most annoyed you about them. Examine their qualities closely. Is it possible that the thing you most dislike in them might be an unacknowledged aspect of yourself? For the next few months, pay attention to the way you respond to people. If you notice yourself feeling annoyed or disgusted by them, look deeper to see if you can learn something useful about yourself from these encounters.

4. Who do you most admire?

As well as reflecting on qualities you find most difficult to deal with, look for qualities you idealise in others too. These are what we might call your 'positive shadow' – the same characteristics that demon-strate the hidden light in you. Think about what you admire most in others, their courage, creativity or wisdom, for example, and make a note of anyone who evokes a feeling of envy. While comparison really can be the thief of joy, it can also motivate us to create positive change in our lives.

Letter writing game

One of my favourite exercises is one Sally Kempton calls the 'letter writing game'. Set aside half an hour to write two letters. The first should be to a person you dislike or disapprove of, describing all of the things that trouble you about them. Express these criticisms as though they're directed right at them, for example, 'I loathe the way you talk over others and often speak about yourself'.

Write the second letter to someone you admire. Note in detail all of the qualities you see in that person, such as, 'I love how calm you are when things are stressful' or 'I admire your confident way of speaking'.

When your letters are finished, read each one in front of the mirror, substituting every 'you' for 'I' and 'your' for 'my'.

Finally, take some time to sit and reflect, breathing into your heart area. As you do this, invite yourself to be open to the qualities you have seen in others and yourself. Allow the dark and light sides of yourself to become more balanced, and as you find acceptance for your shadow self, begin to make room for your light.

Trusting your confident self

A key goal of IFS is to restore a sense of connection and trust in Self energy so it can take the lead in more of our interactions with the world. It's important to remember that within the IFS approach, there are no 'bad' parts. Each aspect of us has formed to either enrich or protect us in some way, and therefore each part is valuable and has worth. It's only when protectors spring into action unnecessarily and make us act out, withdraw or behave in ways that scupper our opportunities that we run into problems.

Strategies that may have helped us as children become outdated and counterproductive, but connecting with your confident self can change everything. As a compassionate, kind, patient energy, it's the only one able to observe the others non-judgementally and mediate between them. It has the power and wisdom to bring harmony to this inner world and can even re-parent the vulnerable parts if given the opportunity.

Bringing harmony to our inner world is incredibly important when building confidence because, whether we know it or not, these selves are running our lives. Most of the time, they exist behind the scenes, triggering reactions and coaxing us into familiar patterns – creating inner and outer conflict in the process. But because their behaviour is so habitual and often repeated, they move us away from the confident self that's within each of us.

Confronting the selves can be uncomfortable

With regular practice, we can develop the ability to pause in the moment between a thought and a reaction. For most of us, the hardest part of any awareness process is remembering to do it in the moment, since we are hardwired to avoid internal discomfort. But it's when we feel irritable, anxious or nervous that we most need to bring awareness to the narratives our minds are linking the situation to.

Pay closer attention to your physical sensations since they offer us so many signals. If we notice tightness in the body, for example, we might see it as a cue to bring awareness to our thoughts, and this strengthens the connection to our wise self. Emotional discomfort is an obvious signal to pause and notice what is happening, but so is feeling numb or disconnected from our emotions, because when some of our emotional needs weren't met in childhood, we may have learned to cut ourselves off from our feelings.

Many clients tell me they've been experiencing this type of disconnection for a long time. If a child doesn't have someone in their life who makes them 'feel felt', they are likely to shut off certain parts of themselves. As an adult, if someone asks them what they are feeling, they may struggle to answer. They've become so used to being in their heads with their thoughts that they've forgotten how to be in their body with their feelings.

A large part of the ACT process (see page 83) is learning how to make room for discomfort so that choice – aka our confident self – can come back into the frame. As therapist Carrie Hayward says, 'Our feelings will do what they do, but if we bring awareness to them and let them be, then we can *choose* to come back to our behaviours; we can be the person we want to be through our actions. This provides a sense of freedom and meaning moment by moment, day by day. And ultimately, in life.' You can find freedom in the ability to *choose* your attitude towards something and what you do and bring attention to. But this is only possible when connected to the confident self.

Take control of the minibus

Given that IFS is a therapy that's difficult to grasp quickly, I often describe this model to clients by inviting them to imagine that this family of selves is packed tightly into a minibus travelling on the highway of life. How smoothly their journey progresses and whether they reach their intended destination largely depends on who is driving.

When we're not feeling sure of ourselves, it might be because one of our inner children is behind the wheel. This vulnerable part might feel helpless or directionless, and say things such as, 'I have no idea what I'm doing or where I'm going.' Because these vulnerable parts are often wounded and full of fear, they are cautious, indecisive and overly concerned about what others think of them.

In moments like these, a protector such as the inner critic might jump in the driver's seat and say things like, 'You're useless. You're not smart enough. You need to do better.' Because our protectors can be rigid and controlling, they're prone to bullying and shouting. But in the same way that this kind of talk doesn't help a child to feel more confident, this is unhelpful, too, for our inner children.

If we're able to access Self energy, we have the capacity to be kind and compassionate with the vulnerable part of ourselves while also being firm and gentle with the overly vigilant protectors. You can imagine politely asking the protector if they'd take another seat on the bus while you take the wheel. In the same way a loving parent would soothe and comfort a real child, you might imagine guiding your inner child to sit beside you or on your lap as you offer them words of comfort and support.

The goal isn't to eliminate the protectors, either – many of them still have important roles to play. Instead, it's about helping them to transition into 'non-extreme' (aka less destructive) roles. When the protector parts learn that the confident self can be trusted to look out for the vulnerable children, they can relax and be less reactive. They might still spring forward out of habit, but the more connected we become to the strong, wise part of us, the less this will happen. Eventually, this calmer, less-reactive environment becomes the new baseline. One of the great benefits of bringing harmony to our inner world is that it allows our inner children to rediscover their innate lightness and joy. When they trust that they are safe and know that they have unconditional love and acceptance, the world becomes less scary. It's a wondrous place full of possibilities again.

Only when you understand who's on the bus and what they need can you start to work *with* these parts and put the wise, confident self in the driver's seat. Through this process, the parts of you that are wounded and damaged can begin to heal.

~

When making a case for healing the parts of us that are fragile, there is a powerful and compelling reason that has nothing to do with how we relate to ourselves, but rather how we relate to other people. When we live in a state of inner conflict and chaos – struggling against our aggressive, defensive protectors – it colours the way we perceive and relate to others. However, when we are able to treat those difficult parts of us with loving compassion and understanding, we are also able to see others this way, too.

Inner harmony makes it possible for us to connect with other people more deeply. We don't just become wiser about ourselves, we become wiser about others and better equipped to spot their vulnerabilities and fears. Strengthening our self-compassion muscle makes us better able to respond to others with the same compassionate clarity we are starting to show ourselves. Creating these ideal conditions for connection is hugely important because, contrary to popular belief, introverts are all about connection.

FOURTEEN

Connect with others

Social connection is not only essential to our survival as a species, it's also vital to our health. In 2019, researchers examining the results of 52 studies involving more than 47,000 participants found that social connection benefits our wellbeing in many ways, including strengthening our immune system and helping us to recover from disease faster. They concluded that people with strong social connections tend to have higher self-esteem and exhibit more empathy for other people. They are also more trusting and cooperative, which in turn means others are more trusting and cooperative towards them. This suggests that social connectedness begets more connection – improving our social, emotional and physical wellbeing in the process. The elderly of Okinawa, Japan, are living proof of how important connectedness is to thriving.

Okinawa is one of the world's 'blue zones' – areas where people tend to live longer and have better lives than almost anywhere else in the world. In Okinawa, several key factors contribute to its people's extraordinary longevity and wellness, but perhaps the most significant is the unique approach to fostering social connection.

In addition to families, friends and work colleagues, Okinawans benefit from the relationships they form in *moai* – small groups that meet regularly for a 'common purpose'. *Moai* have been part of Okinawan life for hundreds of years. Originally, they were formed so people could pool their resources, but they evolved into built-in support systems for everyone in the city.

Children are put into a *moai* with several of their peers when they are young. They make a commitment to each other for life and meet daily or several times a week for the entirety of their lives, forming a sort of secondary family. Often, people will belong to two or more *moai* since groups can form around any shared interest (e.g., cooking, gardening or reading).

When American writer Dan Buettner spoke to dozens of elderly Okinawan residents about the role *moai* had played in their lives, he learned that deep support and respect for each other was fundamental. Klazuko Manna, the youngest in her *moai* at 77 years old, told Buettner what belonging to her *moai* meant to her: 'If you get sick or a spouse dies, or if you run out of money, we know someone will step in and help. It's much easier to go through life knowing there is a safety net.'

This incredible social safety net offers the security of knowing people will come to your aid if you need it – something lacking in many Western countries, such as America, where one-third of people report having fewer than two people to lean on. The people of Okinawa are deeply connected to their community, which provides them with comfort, companionship and frequent interaction. This is something that is missing for so many people, especially as they age, and loneliness creeps in.

It's important to note that loneliness is not the same thing as social isolation, though the two can be related. A person experiencing loneliness usually feels emotionally isolated from other people, even when they are surrounded by people. Social isolation, on the other hand, tends to be situational. It has to do with not seeing or having contact with many people – something many of us experienced during the global pandemic. Sometimes, social isolation can lead to loneliness, as seems to be the case for many Australians.

Many of my clients tell me how lonely they feel. Some long for more friends or a romantic partner, while others report feeling lonely with their families or in marriages of several decades. Though deep bonds such as those with a spouse or close friend can be incredibly meaningful, they are not the only bonds capable of lessening our loneliness and providing life-enhancing benefits.

Finding connection: Camille's story

When Camille's partner Luc was transferred from Paris to Melbourne for work, she was distressed at leaving behind friends and family. Like most of my clients, Camille was loyal to a handful of long-term relationships. The thought of having to start over at building meaningful connections in a city on the other side of the world filled her with anxiety. She felt so overwhelmed that she couldn't even think about where to begin.

Camille and I spoke about taking the emphasis away from 'making good friends' initially and instead, focus on engaging in a few interests and activities so that she could lay the foundation of feeling connected to her new city.

She joined a ceramics class and made the decision to arrive at work an hour early each Wednesday, so she'd have time for a leisurely coffee at a nearby café that housed a large communal table. As it turned out, the coffee mornings became the highlight of her week.

Over the three months we worked together, Camille didn't make a new best friend, but the familiar faces at the café and the occasional conversations with other customers gave her enough informal social contact to stop her from feeling so isolated.

Feeling connected, *within*

Social connection has more to do with our *subjective* feeling of connection than our number of friends. As long as we *feel* we are connected with others, we can still reap the same benefits of actual social connection.

If you've ever had the experience of feeling lonely in a crowd or with some of your friends, you'll likely understand the concept of subjective connection and how it's possible to feel a sense of connection with others *within ourselves* rather than with them. This is good news for those who prefer their own company.

A simple way to generate feelings of connection is by supporting others through activities such as volunteering or giving of yourself to someone else. Even the simple act of getting to know your elderly neighbour and regularly putting her rubbish bins out can build feelings of compassion and create a sense of connection and purpose.

Since high stress levels are also related to higher levels of self-focus, focusing on other people is also a great way to lower stress while also increasing those feelings of connection. One small step you can take to remedy this is to practise self-compassion. The better care you take of yourself, the more likely you are to reach out to others.

Learning to ask for what we need is also a great way of strengthening connection. When we reach out to others for assistance, not only does it help us but it gives others the feeling of being needed.

ALL social ties are lifelines

In a series of studies that looked at the lifestyles of tens of thousands of middle-aged Americans over seven years, researchers found that the two most significant indicators of longevity weren't tied to diet, exercise, cardiac health or even smoking – they were tied to social connections.

The top three indicators of longevity are:

1. **Social integration:** Interactions with people you see daily. These can include weak and strong bonds.
2. **Close relationships:** Your closest friends. The people who support you through bad times.
3. **Drinking/smoking habits:** How often you drink and whether or not you used to (or still) smoke.

The power of social connection is evident in the Sardinian village of Villagrande. Sardinia is one of the original blue zones and the only place in the world where men live as long as women. The layout of the medieval Italian village, with its tightly spaced houses and interwoven streets, forces its residents into closer contact. Their lives are always intersecting, which means that older generations are constantly surrounded by people. Friends, family members, grocers or neighbours – there is always someone to socialise with, even in passing. It's this daily contact with the people in their orbit that ensures the older men live just as long as the older women. In other parts of the world, elderly women tend to gravitate more to other people and continue to foster relationships. Men, on the other hand, are more likely to withdraw, and their quality and length of life suffer as a result.

The knowledge that daily contact can have such a dramatic impact on our health is important information to have. It means that most of us – at least those of us who don't live in the remotest of rural locations – have countless opportunities every day to improve our wellbeing. Though extroverts may be better at engaging in small talk, smiling and saying a quick hello to someone they see daily, this is also well within the capability of even the shyest introvert.

I don't consider myself an overly social person, but one of the upsides of growing up in an extroverted family is that it taught me the importance of regularly engaging with people. Whenever I leave my house, I make an effort to engage briefly with whoever I run into. I might ask the teenager at the grocery checkout if they're looking forward to the school holidays or the barista making my coffee how their morning has been. Throughout the day, I look for small moments of connection. I've always suspected that doing this was good for everyone involved, and now I know that it is. So, it seems, does the Dutch government.

In 2019, after data revealed that over half of Dutch people over 75 regularly felt lonely, the government launched an initiative to combat loneliness. As part of this program, Jumbo, a Dutch supermarket with over 700 stores, trialled a *Kletskassa*, or 'chat checkout' scheme in one of its stores. The dedicated slow lane that was created for customers who weren't in a rush and wanted to chat with a cashier was a success with customers *and* store staff. They also introduced coffee corners in their stores so customers had a spot to sit and have coffee together. The feedback was so positive that Jumbo gave the green light to add another 200 *Kletskassa* to their stores.

Find daily opportunities to connect

As you go about your day, work on bringing more awareness to the people who cross your path. In public spaces, direct your attention to whatever is happening around you. Take a few seconds to ask a colleague how their daughter's dance recital went. Ask the security guard at your office how their weekend was. So many of us are guilty of burying our heads in our phones while waiting in a queue or on the bus, but micro connections such as making eye contact and nodding at a fellow commuter can go a long way to making us all feel more connected.

If you find it challenging to strike up conversations with people you don't know well, start with even smaller actions. Help a parent carry their pram up some stairs at a train station. Hold a door open for someone. Pass the person waiting on your table the dirty dishes they can't quite reach. None of these things require conversation – you can simply smile. Turn it into a game and see how many people you can interact with in the next hour or day. The more we flex these social muscles, the more confident we are about using them.

Loneliness affects introverts just as much as extroverts – arguably even more so, since a lonely extrovert is likely to open themselves to the world by drumming up a conversation with a stranger or putting themselves in social situations where they can forge connections. In contrast, a lonely introvert is far more likely to withdraw and become closed off from the world.

For this reason, introverts need to pay special attention to nurturing connections in order to stave off loneliness and isolation. These social links are crucial to our emotional and physical wellbeing, so we can and should be proactive about them.

For introverts, it's the *quality of the connection*, not the *number of connections*, that matter. As long as we have time to recharge our social batteries, there's no reason any of us should be lonely unless, of course, we feel that we're unable to make a genuine connection. But sometimes introverts put up a protective mask to guard our vulnerable selves and often, we don't even realise we're doing it. However, like many of our protective mechanisms, masks hinder rather than help when trying to forge connections. I'm sure you've probably had the experience of talking to someone but feeling you weren't quite seeing the real them. This often ends our motivation to interact with them, but occasionally we persist and see if we can penetrate their protective veneer.

Many years ago, when my children were little, I met a woman at a mutual friend's dinner party. The two of us got chatting, and it turned out that she lived in my neighbourhood. From time to time, I ran into her at events, but even though I liked her, I found it hard to connect on anything other than a superficial level.

Then, during a summer when many of our mutual friends were away on holiday, we ran into each other in the street and she invited me to join her at a weekly yoga class. For the following year, we walked to yoga every week. One morning, after a tough couple of hours with one of my daughters, I allowed myself to be vulnerable with her. She met my emotion with warm empathy and even shared some vulnerable stories herself. From there, we started to build the most beautiful friendship.

It had taken a while, and I hadn't anticipated the eventual depth of our friendship, but I'm so grateful to have her as a friend. It's a great reminder that we can dismiss one another too quickly when we meet with our masks on. For me and my friend, it took a specific circumstance and the connection point of a family challenge to break down the wall, but we were both willing to be real when the moment presented itself, and that made all the difference.

Whenever I conclude one of my six-day retreats for women, attendees always ask me how I managed to find such beautiful women, and I always answer that people are always beautiful when they are willing to be real and let themselves be seen.

Vulnerability in small doses

In her book *Daring Greatly*, Brené Brown explains that being vulnerable doesn't mean baring your soul or sharing your deepest, darkest secrets. Vulnerability can also be expressed in much smaller ways, such as admitting that you're having a difficult day, like I did with my friend. It might also be asking someone you trust for input or feedback on something you've done. If you find it hard to be vulnerable with people, consider practising by asking someone close to you if they can add to some of the strengths you've already identified. The people who know you well often see you in ways you can't see yourself, so they can shed light on talents and gifts you don't realise you have. By opening up, you'll also be letting that person know that you trust them and that their opinion matters to you because *they* matter. And feeling like we matter to someone is often the beginning of connection.

'Mattering' matters

Importantly, moments of connection with other people don't just make us feel alive; they also make us feel validated and seen. They remind us that we are of value – not only to other people but also to ourselves. *Meaning* might provide the personal impetus to push you beyond your comfort zone, but *mattering* is the fuel that builds connection.

How much we believe we matter is central to how we see ourselves and how we feel about our lives. Someone who thinks they don't matter is likely to lack a basic sense of human connectedness (that sense of feeling connected *within*) as well as a sense of personal significance.

Dr Gordon Flett, who researches and writes about mattering, believes it is a significant marker of wellbeing in all areas of our lives, including home, work and in our communities. He describes mattering as being able to:

- hold the interest and attention of others;
- feel noticed and heard;
- believe someone cares about you and makes you feel special;
- feel valued, cherished and wanted;
- sense that people appreciate you in their lives, not just for what you do, but also for who you are; and
- understand that you'd be missed if you were no longer around.

According to Dr Flett, mattering helps meet our core need for connection, but simply connecting with another person isn't enough to satisfy this need. For this to happen, we need to feel that we're connected *and* valued at the same time.

Researchers have also discovered that mattering has a powerful influence on our actions. When we feel as though we matter, we have a greater sense of agency and the capacity to adapt. We are better able to build resilience in the face of life's challenges, and this makes us more confident in unchartered waters. Mattering also offers protection against negative social influences such as bullying. In short, the more we feel we matter, the more hopeful we are, the higher our executive functioning and the less lonely we become.

The feeling that you aren't important can have a domino effect on many aspects of your life, and this is something researcher Zach Mercurio explores in an article titled, 'How to Create Mattering at Work'. He writes:

> *'When someone doesn't believe they matter at work, it's easy for nothing to matter. People won't share their voice if they don't believe their voice is significant. People won't use their strengths if they don't believe they have strengths. People won't contribute if they don't believe they have something to contribute. People won't care until they feel cared for.'*

It's clear that if we want to engage with the world and other people, and access our inner confidence, it isn't enough to value ourselves – we need to believe that we matter to others as well. Hopefully, you already trust that you *do* matter – as we all do – but in case you don't, let's explore how to change that.

How to feel like you matter: Luke's story

It's hard to feel confident or hopeful when we don't feel connected to others, and since these feelings often lead to a low mood state, the assumption that we don't matter to others can become exaggerated.

Some time ago, a kind and creative client named Luke told me that he'd spent several stretches of time in hospital, diagnosed with serious clinical depression. When all of this took place, Luke's relationship had broken down, he was experiencing financial difficulty and he'd lost touch with many of his friends. 'I didn't feel like I mattered to anyone,' he told me. 'I felt like I was a burden and depressing to be around. I thought that it would be a relief for people to be rid of me and that no one was going to miss me.'

It was painful to hear Luke's stark admission, but this wasn't the first time I'd heard someone share a story of the kind of pain that makes it more appealing to no longer be here. In an increasingly isolated society, we're more at risk of feeling that we don't belong. Luke's experience reflects the findings of a 2023 study, which revealed that 33 per cent of Australians are currently experiencing loneliness, putting them at greater risk of disease, addiction, anxiety and depression. Worryingly, 58 per cent of this group reported not speaking up about their loneliness. Many say they feel ashamed about it and 'less worthy' as a result.

But, as Luke found during his recovery in hospital, his assumption had been wrong. Old friends started to reach out, and once he settled into a new home, he was more open with people when he needed company. Once the cycle of loneliness was broken, he also found the energy to proactively seek out new connections.

Mattering is a reciprocal experience

The research tells us that the pathway to mattering is to *have value to others* and to *give value to others*. We know that in order to break the cycle of loneliness and feel some connection, we need to take small steps to reach out to others and to build relationships that will help us feel we have a meaningful place in the lives of others. We can do this by volunteering or mentoring someone, or by connecting over shared interests. In Luke's case, a local tennis club became a safe haven. After a few weeks, one of the members invited him to join them for coffee and later, they organised a group dinner. Luke's natural inclination was to avoid too much social contact and initially he declined. His teammate followed up with a phone call, offering to pick Luke up so they could arrive at dinner together and Luke felt touched by this small thoughtful gesture. The regular (but not too regular) catch-ups with these new friends felt manageable, while also giving him the sense that he mattered.

Here are some simple ways to let people know that they matter to you:

- Spend undistracted time with them. This is one of the easiest ways to let someone know you genuinely value them.
- Be a great listener and let people know they've been heard.
- When someone has been away, let them know they were missed.
- Make an effort to remember things that are important to others (birthdays, interests, the names of their children).
- Model and encourage giving to people.

It's equally important to be aware of the small things that can make others feel insignificant. These are sometimes referred to as 'anti-mattering practices', and they include the following behaviours:

- Criticising.
- Using sarcasm.

- Talking over people.
- Looking at your phone when they are speaking.
- Not paying attention when they are talking to you.
- Using social comparisons.
- Being too distracted when you're with people.

The power of micro connections

Clients often tell me that they want to build confidence when it comes to dealing with other people. They want to feel more at ease when speaking with others, become better at advocating for themselves or improve their networking skills, since this is a job requirement that often trips up ambitious introverts.

One of the reasons we find connecting with others intimidating is because we build it up to be something big in our heads. Scaling back the expectations we have of ourselves is a solid first step towards building our confidence in this area. It's unlikely you'd even want to sweep into a room and wow a crowd in order to make connections. The key to success is playing to your introvert strengths.

I recommend starting with small and subtle connections and building from there. Remember, the fear response in our brain is much less likely to be triggered if we take small actions that don't alert it to change. I don't consider myself a natural when it comes to public speaking, however, I've come to accept that it's an important way of sharing my knowledge, so I've found strategies to become more comfortable on stage. One tiny thing that's been very helpful is making micro connections with people in the crowd prior to giving a talk.

Before each event, I stand in the room as the audience files in, and while I don't say much, I smile at people or help someone find a seat. Occasionally, I'll say a quick hello and introduce myself. These are such small actions that they're easy for me to do, but once I'm in front of people, these little investments really pay off. I feel less isolated when I'm able to look out and see one or two friendly faces. Don't underestimate the impact baby steps like these can have on helping you feel more at ease and confident in yourself.

Taking the pressure out of a conference: Amy's story

Amy, a client, works in tech and travels to the US a few times a year to attend conferences. One-on-one, she's warm and engaging, but in large groups, she finds it hard to find her feet. Like many introverts, Amy finds making small talk difficult, so in the lead-up to yet another conference, she began to explore ways to improve her experience.

As luck would have it, she was invited to join a WhatsApp group for women in her field who would also be attending. With 15 women on the chat, for the first few days, Amy stayed pretty quiet, but as the conversation progressed to restaurants to visit in Seattle, she introduced herself and suggested a few places she'd read about. As the group continued exchanging messages over the next couple of weeks, Amy found herself warming up and even looking forward to meeting these women.

When she returned to Australia, Amy told me how much she'd enjoyed the conference, and it was clear that these new connections had been a big reason for that. 'We met up at a restaurant on the first afternoon,' she said, 'and it felt like we'd known each other for ages.' Another benefit for Amy was discovering that she wasn't the only person who found these events nerve-racking: 'We talked a lot about how awkward these conferences can be, and it was nice to know that other people felt the same way I did.'

This experience of 'pre-connecting' increased Amy's confidence and helped her realise that she didn't have to play an extrovert's game to survive these conferences in future. She became much more enthusiastic about attending events and growing her professional network. Used judiciously, groups like these increase the likelihood that we'll feel safe enough to put down our masks and engage on a real level, face-to-face, which is where introverts come into their own.

Pre-connect to connect

The next time you find yourself facing a new situation you feel nervous about, consider how you can pre-connect with other people to take some of the pressure out of it. If you are moving to a new city, look online to find local groups. If you have a dog, join the neighbourhood's Facebook group and ask where the best local dog parks are. If you're attending a big event, like Amy, ask the organiser if there's a group for attendees you can join (or even start), and then introduce yourself once you join. You won't be the only person who's feeling nervous about the upcoming event and eager to make a friend.

If there's no route to connect prior to an event, do some homework ahead of time so you at least know who you'd like to meet and talk to. Once at the event, remind yourself that you don't have to meet every person. There will be extroverts 'working the room' and collecting contacts, but that is their thing, not yours. Save your energy and attention for the people you most want to talk to. Genuine conversation and interest will always be more memorable than small talk.

Use digital tools to your advantage

If networking or growing your influence is important in your work, leveraging digital resources and social media can help you play to your strengths. The virtual world can put us in front of many people while also providing us with the space we need to choose our words carefully and consider how much of ourselves we are comfortable sharing.

The digital revolution has given many introverts a chance to step into positions of influence they might never have pursued in the physical world. From the comfort of their living rooms, introverts with good ideas can decide when and with whom they engage. They can also connect with like-minded people over shared passions, interests and opinions without feeling they need to act like an extrovert or compete to be heard. They have the chance to let others get to know them (at least virtually) on their own terms. In some ways, this echoes the 'village-like' mindset that typified early Western culture, where authenticity and character were the currency that increased a person's influence.

There's no substitute for contact IRL

While technology can help us find our people, at the same time there's an overwhelming amount of research pointing to the way our digital existence is fuelling feelings of social isolation. We know that social media use can be detrimental to the mental health of users, especially younger people who don't do enough socialising in real life. Texting and messaging online are great, but they're no substitute for human contact.

Science shows that face-to-face contact causes our brains to release neurotransmitters that help foster trust, reduce stress, kill pain and induce pleasure. The protective qualities of this neuro-chemical response benefit us in the moment of contact *and* long after. In brain scans, neuroscientists have demonstrated that this response cannot be replicated through digital connection. We need to have face-to-face contact to trigger these complex responses and reap their associated benefits.

Connection summary

- Identifying and focusing on your unique strengths is a powerful confidence-boosting exercise.
- Introverts and highly sensitive people have many unique strengths of their own.
- Each of us already has a 'confident' part of ourselves within – as well as other parts that often inhibit confidence.
- Social connection is not just good for confidence, it's vital to our health (even for introverts).
- Mattering to other people has a powerful impact on how we feel about ourselves and it also influences our actions. Both things significantly impact our confidence.

Part Three

Courage

I've heard it said that we are in the midst of an 'overthinking epidemic', and given the rise of mental health conditions such as anxiety, depression and loneliness since the global pandemic, this seems pretty accurate. Aside from the challenges overthinking creates, it does nothing for our confidence. If anything, it's very likely to sap it. Excessive rumination is also linked to poorer mental health.

In the first part of this book, I wrote about the study where women and men were given the same test, and women opted out of answering the questions they weren't sure of. The men performed better, not because they were smarter, but because they answered all of the questions. In the next round, when instructed to complete every answer, the women did as well as the men, leading to the conclusion that action is *the* most crucial aspect of building confidence.

Transforming an idea, intention, goal or dream into something tangible only becomes possible once we *commit to take action*.

Deciding about which action to take is where people with low confidence often struggle, especially if they have perfectionist tendencies. Their fear of making the wrong decision or not being able to take 'good enough' action either keeps them stuck in a cycle of rumination or leads them to avoid the situation entirely. If this sounds familiar, take comfort in the knowledge that our decision-making skills can be practised and improved at any point in our lives.

Most people agree that *any* decision is better than no decision, so if you find yourself feeling stuck or scared, remember that doing nothing constitutes a decision in itself, and the consequences of inaction can be equally as bad as (if not worse than) doing the wrong thing. Ignoring the lump in your breast, putting your parking fines in the drawer rather than paying them right away, not taking a new partner's propensity for violence seriously or, like Hannah the lawyer, letting yourself become physically sick before leaving a role are decisions that can be significantly harmful.

If this doesn't encourage you to be more decisive, think about who you are when you are being the best version of yourself. Do you pause before acting because you're cautious about doing the wrong thing? Or, do you make the best decision you can based on the information available and take action? Both of these 'best selves' are making a decision, but only one is displaying courage.

FIFTEEN

What is courage?

The Western notion of courage shares a lot of the same extroverted, masculine undertones as the Western idea of confidence. This may have something to do with the portrayal of 'courageous' characters in traditional myths, stories and movies. Though females make appearances more frequently these days, overwhelmingly, the cast of courageous characters we've been presented with have been male, and the action they've taken has been bold and dramatic (usually in the face of mortal danger).

Just as it was with confidence, this type of courage is not the only flavour on the menu. If you've ever been in love, parented a child, owned up to a mistake or stepped outside a comfort zone, you already understand that life is constantly demanding that we take courageous action, and that courage comes in all shapes and sizes.

More recently, the definition of courage has broadened to include 'softer', more humane types of courage, thanks in part to Brené Brown's groundbreaking research on shame, courage and vulnerability, and her ability to translate these findings into easily accessible books, Netflix specials and TED Talks. Brown's willingness to be vulnerable herself and her brilliant capacity for storytelling mean that these topics have become mainstream, and we understand, more than ever, how they inform our behaviour.

While calling to us during moments that require true bravery, courage lives in the quiet and intimate moments of our lives too. Being vulnerable with another person, for example, can require extraordinary courage, as does accepting the risk of heartbreak, embarrassment or failure and forging ahead regardless. The evaluation of risk and the decision to proceed is the greatest difference between courage and bravery.

The difference between bravery and courage

These two words are often used interchangeably, but there is a subtle, important distinction between them. Bravery involves acting with a strong sense of confidence and an absence of fear. A brave person accepts a challenge and takes bold action without necessarily weighing up the pros and cons first. In their mind, the challenge is one they have the ability to tackle.

A courageous person tends to think and evaluate the risk *before* taking action. When they do act, it's in spite of their fear, not in the absence of it. Unlike their brave counterparts, they usually act without complete confidence that they will be successful. Instead, they determine that the outcome is worth the risk, and they take heart-led action.

Courage is born in the heart

The word 'courage' comes from the Latin word *cor* (heart), and one of the earliest definitions of courage is 'to speak one's mind by telling all one's heart'. Speaking from the heart is what Brené Brown refers to as 'ordinary courage'.

I love the term 'ordinary courage' because it flies in the face of the expectation for courage to be bold or exceptional. It reminds us that 'ordinary' things – the laughter of a child, a supremely fluffy soufflé or pinky-red sunrise – are frequently extraordinary. In my mind, ordinary courage *is* extraordinary because it has the power to make us take action in relation to things we care deeply about: family, friends or perhaps certain values, beliefs or dreams we hold dear.

When people tell me about themselves, I listen carefully to the words that they choose to describe themselves. Frequently, the word 'fearful' comes up more often than 'courageous', and when it does, I explain that taking fear-led action in the past doesn't mean a person is destined to always do this. Fear drives a lot of human behaviour – often subconsciously – and there's no shame in this because fear is powerful, but so is courage.

Chances are, courage is behind a good amount of behaviour even for those who do not evaluate themselves as being courageous. When prompted, the same clients are often surprised to realise they can identify plenty of times when they've demonstrated this type of ordinary courage. Whether it was letting their partner know their feelings had been hurt, or asking a work colleague for help, every small courageous action counts because action begets more action and ultimately, many of these actions will improve your confidence.

Opening to vulnerability: Ravi's story

Some years ago, Ravi came to me for help understanding and communicating his feelings. For several years, his wife, Nicki, had been trying to get him to open up to her, and had often told him that she wanted them to communicate more. Recently, however, Ravi had noticed that Nicki was making less of an effort to engage with him. He was concerned that the distance between them was growing, and he was desperate to change that before it was too late.

Ravi told me that he'd grown up with a domineering and intolerant father. In his childhood home, vulnerability of any kind was likely to lead to being ridiculed or bullied into 'toughening up'. Hiding his vulnerabilities had been an effective coping strategy back then, but ultimately, Ravi had become so disconnected from his emotions that he struggled to even name what he felt, let alone express it.

Unfortunately, Ravi's difficulty connecting with Nicki was a fairly common example of what happens when we withdraw from people, or when we hide our true selves because we feel shame or vulnerability. In order to be open with other people, we need to find ways of feeling safe with them – something Ravi hadn't felt growing up.

I explained that before opening up to Nicki, he would first have to reconnect with his feelings. I suggested he start with a brief meditation each morning. He committed to this, and sat in stillness for five minutes upon waking, bringing awareness to the sensations in his body and reflecting on what those might be trying to tell him. Initially, he found this process uncomfortable, but he stayed with it and began building an all-important awareness.

A few weeks into this practice, Ravi had a significant communication breakthrough with his wife. After recounting an argument he'd had with a work colleague earlier that day, Nicki asked him how the encounter had made him feel. He wasn't sure, but rather than avoid the question, he chose to exercise ordinary courage and be vulnerable.

For the first time, he was honest about how hard he found it to name his emotions. To his relief, his wife didn't make a big deal about this, or make him feel that he was abnormal. Instead, she helped by gently naming a few emotions she suspected he might have felt. 'His behaviour sounds incredibly frustrating,' she said. 'It must have been hurtful and disappointing for you.'

Sharing with Nicki in this way gave Ravi confidence to be more vulnerable with her in the future. He told me that this one simple conversation had already created a deeper connection between him and his wife.

What sparks (ordinary) courage in you?

What courageous action have you taken recently? Remember, courage is expressed when we feel fear but take action anyway. These moments don't have to be momentous (though they might be). Ordinary courage counts, too. Write down a few examples of when you've been courageous. You'll probably find you can think of at least a dozen of these once you get going, but if you get stuck, revisit the list of achievements you made in '(Re)connect to your confident self' on page 151.

Next, review your list and ask yourself *why* you were able to take each of these actions. What was it that gave you the strength to override the accompanying fear? Often, our values and purpose are hiding in plain sight, spurring us to act despite our fears. In Ravi's case, his value of connection and his desire to build a stronger relationship with his wife gave him the courage to be vulnerable.

Can you list the values or sources of meaning that gave you the strength to overcome your fears? How might you be able to use these even more effectively in the future? Reminding ourselves of these sources of power makes it easier for us to access courage when we need it.

You might also like to see courage as one of your values (see pages 80–3). This way, the goal is no longer *being* courageous, it's *choosing to act* in a courageous way in the moment. Living in alignment with the value of courage makes it more likely that you will take action in the direction of your goals and dreams. When you do, you can feel good about your efforts regardless of the outcome.

With this in mind, I invite you to change your mindset around the idea of courage: don't think of it as a quality you either have or don't have. Think of it as a habit you build over time. Quiet courage breeds quiet confidence because when you act from your purpose and values, trusting your own judgement becomes second nature. Through the process of looking inwards rather than outwards for answers, tuning in to your heart and listening to the wisest part of yourself, you'll discover that you *are*, in fact, a courageous person.

Why is it so important that we practise courage?

Courage is what allows us to stretch beyond our limitations and evolve. Comfort zones can easily get too comfortable and once we're in one – whether it's at work, in a relationship or creatively – the last thing we feel like doing is abandoning that safe space to do something that scares us. But if we want our lives to change and progress in all the ways we dream of, this is exactly what needs to happen – again and again throughout our lives. Often it can take a few attempts to successfully break out of a comfort zone, but only by challenging ourselves in small ways and taking calculated risks can we become more fully rounded (and more confident) individuals.

On a primal level, each of us already understands that it's essential to stretch ourselves sometimes, because this is how we've each amassed the skills we currently possess. From childhood, life presents us with new opportunities masked as 'scary' challenges at every turn – our first day of school, learning to ride a bike, going on a first date. Only by taking one courageous action after another do we discover that we are so much more capable than we realised, and that the things we feared often aren't so bad after all. (A lot of them are even surprisingly fun!)

As children, it's our parents, teachers, older siblings and friends who guide us towards the unknown and encourage us to take courageous action, but no matter how much they want us to grow, they can't *do* the thing for us. Progress is only made once *we* make the choice to move forwards. As adults, the responsibility falls on us to continue pushing ourselves so we don't plateau. If we're lucky, we might have an encouraging partner or supportive group of friends to nudge us out of our comfort zone now and then, but we can't rely on other people for all our future growth.

Inside each of us is a database full of experiences where we've stepped outside a comfort zone. Recalling these as we did in the exercise earlier is a great way of reminding ourselves that some of the best rewards in life live just on the other side of a seemingly daunting challenge. And with every small success, we don't just learn something new, we bolster our sense of self-worth and build more trust in our own ability to *try*.

The deep, abiding confidence we're seeking to build is strengthened when we act with courage and it becomes an internal engine propelling us towards the next moment of growth. Once a challenge is realised, this increases our confidence, which we can draw from for the next courageous action, which in turn increases our confidence yet again. This courage–confidence loop strengthens with every action you take, and you can trigger it today by starting in the smallest of ways. When taken consistently, tiny courageous actions can compound, creating dramatic changes over the long term.

What small courageous action could you take today?

- Could you say hi to the person you see in your Pilates class each week?
- Could you apologise to a friend or family member for something that's been hanging over your head?
- Could you be honest with your boss and let them know that you are feeling overwhelmed by your workload?
- Could you take one small step to market your small business?
- Could you accept responsibility for your role in an argument or a break-up?
- Could you join an art class, even though you're a true beginner?
- Could you update your CV or LinkedIn profile to truly celebrate your achievements?
- Could you show a little more of your true self?

Dealing with conflict

Just as we can't spend our lives running from every opportunity that scares us, we can't run from difficult situations, either. These, too, can help us learn and grow.

Unfortunately, many of us have been raised to be polite people-pleasers who avoid confrontation and awkward situations at all costs. This probably made us pliable and more amenable children, but in adulthood, it puts us at a distinct disadvantage – especially if we don't have the vocabulary or experience to stand up for ourselves.

When this is the case, even the smallest disagreement or threat of conflict can trigger our fear response, resulting in us either becoming emotionally charged or shutting down. If this feels familiar, you're not alone. Recent research suggests that introverts are nearly three times more likely than extroverts to want to avoid conflict. The good news is that these skills can be learned and implemented right away. And with each conflict (or 'each opportunity to gain clarity in a relationship') – no matter how minor – you'll become better at staying in the moment, listening to what others are saying and speaking from the part of yourself that is wise, grounded in values and non-reactive.

When we're able to think and speak from this secure place, we are much more likely to engage in 'clean conflict'. By this, I mean we stick to the reality of the situation and not what we imagine it to be. We don't accuse or say hurtful things that we can't take back. To improve the possibility of a clean conflict, try to give yourself some time and space to think beforehand – not just about what you want to say, but also to reflect on the other party's perspective and the outcomes you're hoping to achieve. When you approach a conflict or person with a clear goal in mind, it's more likely the outcome will be constructive rather than destructive.

When dealing with difficult people or situations

- Keep an open, curious mind.
- Assume the best of the other person. Rather than thinking about how important it is to get them to see your point of view, recognise that they probably have valid reasons for their opinions too (just as you do).
- Listen for their real concerns. What are they *really* saying? What really matters to them?
- Use 'I' statements to express your point of view and keep your statements flexible and not permanent.
- After hearing the other person out, try not to react from an emotional place. Give yourself time to respond thoughtfully. Ask for a moment if you need it.
- Throughout the discussion, focus on being present and staying in the moment. Put your energy into staying centred, especially if you notice yourself feeling triggered by the situation. Take a few breaths if you need to.

For me, the final tip on this list is the most important to embody, not only when navigating conflict, but in any setting where I want to feel confident. Learning how to access the calm, centred version of ourselves is a skill that can be learned (even if never really 'perfected'). In the fourth and final part of the book, we'll explore how to strengthen these skills by practising them every day.

How to have a difficult conversation

1. Address conflicts early

As you get better at speaking from the confident part of yourself, do your best not to let small conflicts fester. If you notice tension between you and another person, try to address it as soon as possible to prevent escalation and minimise negative impacts on your relationships.

2. Separate the person from the problem

Remember that resolving conflict is not about assigning blame but rather finding a way to move forward harmoniously. When you do engage, try to focus on staying calm and expressing your opinions with compassion. By focusing on the problem rather than attacking the person, you may find that you can collaborate to find a solution.

3. Choose the right time and place

Addressing an issue while one of the reactive parts of you is driving the minibus will only make things worse. If you can, remove yourself from the situation until you can invite your confident self to come to the fore. Find an appropriate setting and the right moment for both of you to engage in a conversation. This might require asking the other person if there's a time that works for them, rather than launching into conversation unexpectedly or when time is short.

4. Foster open communication

Actively seek out the other person's point of view and keep being open and curious in your discussion. Appeal to your collective objectives rather than the individualistic goal of winning the argument.

5. Practise active listening

Actively listen by showing empathy, being curious and asking clarifying questions. For example, if a family member frequently causes a scene at family get-togethers, find time to catch up one on one and ask them how they're feeling. You might say something like: 'I've noticed that you weren't yourself during dinner. Did anything happen to make you feel that way?'

When the other person responds, paraphrase their answer to ensure you understand their perspectives fully. For example, if your relative were to answer: 'Uncle Joe made several jokes at my expense, and I'm sick of being the family punching bag.' You might follow up by saying: 'So, what I'm hearing is that you feel that Joe's comments and the response from others make you feel that the family is ganging up on you. I understand why that's upsetting. What can I do to help?'

6. Seek common ground

Even when there are differences of opinion, there are bound to be at least one or two areas where there is agreement. Use these to build a foundation for finding solutions and resolving the conflict.

7. Collaborate for win–win outcomes

Foster a cooperative mindset and decide which areas you already agree upon. Work together to aim to find a mutually beneficial solution. Brainstorm and explore alternative options that might be satisfying outcomes for both of you.

8. Remain calm and composed

Do your best to stay calm and composed during discussions where there's conflict. This is easier said than done, but managing your emotions will ensure you don't react or say things impulsively that exacerbate the situation. If needed, take a timeout, but let the other person know when you'll be returning to continue the conversation.

9. Use 'I' statements

When expressing your concerns or perspectives, use 'I' statements to take ownership of your feelings and experiences. This approach avoids blaming or accusing others, fostering a more productive conversation. For example, instead of saying, 'You're always so irritable and snappy during family gatherings,' try 'I felt hurt when you spoke sharply to me at lunch today.'

10. Practise empathy
Shift your perspective and be generous with your assumptions about what others are thinking or feeling. Put yourself in the shoes of the other person and try to understand their feelings, needs and motivations. Demonstrating empathy and compassion helps build trust and facilitates finding common ground.

11. Involve a neutral third party, if necessary
If the conflict persists or becomes highly contentious, consider involving a neutral third party. A skilled therapist or counsellor might be able to offer an objective perspective and help facilitate resolution.

12. Learn from every conflict
Reflect on the underlying causes and dynamics of conflict in your relationships to identify potential areas for improvement in communication.

Setting boundaries

Even though identifying our emotional and physical boundaries and communicating them to others are essential life skills, this is another area of adult life that many of us feel ill-equipped for. All of our relationships benefit when we set and maintain healthy boundaries. Counterintuitively, it's often harder to set boundaries with the people we are closest to. Usually this is because we have fallen into certain patterns and habits with each other, and changing those requires patience and care on both sides.

There are many benefits to establishing boundaries, especially when they are communicated clearly and you make a habit of upholding them. Being clear about your limits allows you to communicate your needs, removing the likelihood of resentment in your relationships.

The courage to set boundaries: Rosie's story

Rosie was one of those people. After almost every dinner with her partner's family, she came home with a knot of frustration and hurt in her stomach. Having been with Matt for five years, she tried to convince herself that she enjoyed spending time with his family, but the reality was, she didn't. Matt's mother, Di, often made passive comments about Rosie's work in a migrant support service and spoke glowingly about Matt's ex-partner, Audrey, a lawyer. Rosie didn't know how to respond to Di and she felt sure she was being too sensitive. Each week before dinner she told herself, 'I need to stop taking this so personally.'

It wasn't until Rosie began experiencing insomnia that she finally began to take her feelings about her mother-in-law more seriously. 'I've realised this is a pattern for me. I never stand up for myself or share my true feelings when I'm hurt,' she told me. 'I think it's time I learned how to because this is really taking a toll on my wellbeing.'

Growing up with a people-pleasing mother, Rosie had frequently been told to not to make a fuss, not to show anger or irritation and not to be so sensitive. As a result, she had learned to stuff down her feelings and choose 'being nice' over 'authenticity'.

Rosie knew it would take some time to change the patterns that had been with her for years. She started working with a therapist who encouraged her to begin by being more open with Matt, who had no idea how she'd been feeling. Matt offered to speak to his mum on her behalf, but Rosie wanted to feel empowered to do this herself. After role-playing scenarios with her therapist, the following week at dinner, Matt's mum made a comment about Audrey's recent promotion. Summoning all of her courage, Rosie spoke honestly about her feelings. 'I wonder if we could avoid conversations about Audrey when we're here, Di,' she asked. 'I find it difficult to hear about what she's doing.'

While under the table her hands were shaking and she felt the familiar knot in her stomach, by next morning Rosie felt something had shifted. 'I still didn't sleep well,' she told me later. 'But when I went for a walk the next morning, I felt a strange kind of opening in my chest. Like I could breathe properly all of a sudden and somewhere within me, I felt a real sense of pride. I stood up for myself! It was terrifying at the time but I can see that this is the beginning of something new for me.'

When we connect to our infinite worth and trust that we are every bit as valuable and lovable as the next person, setting boundaries becomes easier. Requesting to be treated with kindness, respect and consideration is one of the most positive things you can do for yourself and your relationships.

If you haven't given much thought to your own boundaries, becoming aware of how you feel around the people in your life can be a useful starting point. Our body alerts us when our boundaries are crossed, so pay attention to emotions such as anger, frustration or sadness, and be curious about things such as tightness in the body or headaches. The more you notice bodily sensations, the easier it becomes to pinpoint what's causing them, and from there, you can start to outline problematic patterns in a relationship and ask for changes.

If you avoid setting boundaries because you are worried about having a disagreement or conflict of some sort, remember that studies have linked toxic and repressed feelings to ill health and mental health issues. Not speaking up for yourself saps energy and depletes confidence, and eventually, those negative feelings will find a way to be expressed. The passive-aggressive venom that builds up when our boundaries are repeatedly crossed is far more subversive and damaging to a relationship than calm, considered honesty, not to mention far more likely to create an atmosphere that ignites conflict.

If you're new to these conversations, start small and initiate them when you are feeling calm but courageous. If you live in a share house, your first boundary might be asking your house-mate not to leave their dirty dishes in the sink every night. If a friend or family member is always asking to borrow money, let them know you're unable to help this time. If a colleague at work constantly speaks over you, be prepared to say, 'I haven't quite finished yet.' Reasonable requests such as these don't require emotional conversations, lengthy excuses or aggression of any type. Expressing yourself honestly by letting others know how you want to be treated goes a long way to preventing the toxic build-up of energy that occurs when our opinions and needs are routinely ignored.

How to set boundaries

Setting healthy boundaries is essential for maintaining your well-being and building healthy relationships.

1. Know your priorities. To effectively set boundaries, it's essential to understand your own needs, limitations, priorities and values. Self-awareness is the foundational step in this process.

2. Communicate your boundaries clearly. Express your boundaries to others in a clear, consistent and assertive way. As Brené Brown says, the more precise you can be about boundary setting, the more likely it is that your boundaries will be respected.

3. Be consistent. Once you've established an important boundary, try to uphold it consistently. This will help others understand and respect your limits.

4. Extend boundaries to all aspects of life. Boundaries shouldn't be limited to personal relationships. Establish them in your professional life, social interactions, and even in your relationship with technology and social media.

5. Master the art of saying no. Saying no is an important aspect of setting boundaries. Feel that you have the right to politely decline requests or invitations that don't align with your needs or values without getting into detailed explanations.

6. Be aware of feeling guilty. Setting boundaries can often trigger feelings of guilt, especially if you're accustomed to prioritising others over yourself. Remember that taking care of your own needs is not a selfish act but rather, a sign of self-respect.

A recipe for courage

Though I hesitate to frame courage as something that can be achieved by following a simple formula, a common pattern has emerged among the people I've worked with over the years.

Action + feedback + self-reflection = courage

When combined in this particular order, these three processes yield increased courage, and often spark what I call a 'courage loop'. When we take courageous action (large or small) then request feedback on it – not just from other people but also from ourselves – we grow in tiny but meaningful ways. And by reflecting thoughtfully on the experience and how we feel about it, we can decide how much or how little of the external feedback we are going to take on board and whether the goals we've chosen are still right for us.

Each time we cycle through this process, we build trust in our ability to take courageous action, receive feedback and decide what the next action will be. This adds to our reserve of courage, which in turn fuels our next courageous action, and so the loop continues.

Ingredient 1: Action

Several years ago, after determining that my purpose was helping people, I accepted that speaking in front of an audience was an excellent way to reach a wider group. Until this point, I'd declined every speaking invitation I'd received, but once this seed of purpose took root, I couldn't shake the feeling that speaking was something I had to do, or at least try to do.

I decided to accept the next speaking invitation as long as it aligned with my purpose. Before that opportunity arose, I had already drafted an email to say 'yes'. When the request came in, I hit send on that email before I could change my mind. That small action set this new experiment in motion. All I had to do now was complete the rest of the required steps to make this first talk a success.

I committed to going into this talk with as much curiosity and as little fear as I could manage. *Okay*, I thought, *I'm starting here. I'm not experienced at public speaking, but I am interested in it because it supports my purpose. I'm going to give this talk and do the best I can.*

My first time on stage was intimidating and scary, and though I'd secretly hoped I might become a naturally charismatic speaker once I got going, I knew this was unlikely to happen. I tightened under the gaze of the audience and delivered my message directly and plainly. I knew I hadn't completely nailed my presentation but I was satisfied with the effort I'd put in, and while I felt drained from the energy it had taken, I was proud that I'd finally put myself out there.

Break goals into micro steps

Reflect back on the goals you set on page 140 and if you haven't already done so, break each of them down into much smaller steps. Each of these micro steps should be small enough that you can tackle it quickly, and while many will be simple to tick off, it's likely that a few might still seem daunting. These are the most valuable steps because they require courageous action, and by attempting to complete them (in spite of your fear), you are practising courage, and compounding the trust you have in yourself to do hard things.

Micro steps in action: Ivy's story

A couple of years ago, while catching up with Ivy, a friend from my university days, I was surprised to learn that she had competed in several open ocean races. I'd never known her to be a dedicated swimmer, or exerciser, for that matter, and was fascinated to hear how this had come about.

Ivy explained that she'd been looking for something to help her break out of a mental and emotional rut after going through a divorce. She tried tennis, yoga and running, but hadn't enjoyed them enough to continue. A friend told her about a swimming group that met at the beach on Saturday mornings in the spring and summer. After an open-water swim, he said they had coffee on the beach together. According to him, it was good fun, great exercise and the best way to start the weekend. Ivy was intrigued, and with his encouragement, she decided to try it. She even signed up for a two-kilometre ocean swim at the end of the year to give her an incentive to stick with it.

Together, Ivy and her friend put together a gentle but regular training schedule. If she stayed consistent, she'd be strong enough for ocean swimming by the spring. She started small, with two 15-minute swims a week at her local indoor pool. After two months, she increased her training days and times, and in the spring bought her first wetsuit and braved the cold seawater with the swimming group. That first swim was hard, but after, she said she was 'buzzing with happiness, and totally hooked'.

For Ivy, purchasing an online pass for the pool was easy and so was deciding which mornings she would swim. What *wasn't* easy was going to the pool the first few times. 'It was so intimidating,' she said. 'There were way more people there than I expected, and most of them were really good swimmers. I didn't know which swimming lanes I was allowed to use or what the etiquette was when there were multiple people in a lane.' After watching the other swimmers for a few minutes, Ivy slipped back into the change rooms and left without swimming. 'I was worried I'd be too slow and annoy everyone. I just couldn't do it.'

I understood why Ivy had felt this way, and what impressed me was that she didn't let that hiccup derail her plans: 'When I left without swimming, I told myself that this visit was a practice run for the next day. That way, I didn't feel like a failure because I'd worked out where the change rooms were, and I also realised that I needed goggles and a cap, which hadn't occurred to me earlier.'

The next morning, Ivy walked out of the changing room and straight into the pool without hesitation. She struggled through eight slow laps, but nobody seemed to notice. Within two weeks, Ivy said she wasn't giving those morning laps a second thought. 'I just jumped in, swam and then got on with my day.' She'd mastered the first and most intimidating steps in her challenge and had already set her sights on the next one.

Ingredient 2: Feedback

After undertaking whatever action it is we've set our mind to, we can invite feedback on our performance. Opening yourself up to input from other people – especially when trying something new – takes a great deal of courage. It's important to receive whatever comes your way as objectively as possible – something you'll be better able to do when connected to the wise part of you that understands that this journey is about progress, not perfection.

The type of feedback you get will largely depend on the action you've undertaken. If you ran your first 10K, a personal trainer or fellow runner might offer their assessment and some suggestions, or your time might help you gauge how you did. If your courageous action was telling someone you care about that they hurt your feelings, your feedback will be how well they responded to and understood your feelings.

Initially, the feedback I got on my speaking style was not overly positive. I was told that I 'wasn't very entertaining', and that this was something I needed to work on. This dented my confidence, but I reminded myself that this was just my starting point. With more experience, I would improve, but equally, I realised that being 'entertaining' wasn't my most primary objective. I knew I could do better at speaking but what *I* wanted to focus on most was making a better connection with my audience. Feedback is helpful when it tells you how you need to improve, but it's equally helpful in letting you know which parts to discard.

At each stage of the courage journey, it's important to keep the principles of a growth mindset front of mind. Our talents and skills are not fixed. By repeating an action, it's entirely possible to create new neural pathways and improve incrementally each time, but first, you must decide whether the action is worth repeating, and that requires self-reflection.

Ingredient 3: Self-reflection

You're not obliged to take on all of the feedback that comes your way or even agree with it, but I recommend at least considering whether any of it is valid. After reflecting on the feedback on my speaking style, I had to decide what was most important to me. The anxiety leading up to the event had been distracting, and the fear right before stepping on stage was very uncomfortable. After initially hearing the feedback my first thought was, *Perhaps giving talks isn't for me. The emotional cost is too great.* But after brief consideration, I came back to the question of how else I could reach a similar number of people in order to serve my purpose, and decided that it was worth pursuing after all.

With years of practice, my delivery has improved and so has my confidence. Though I'm much more relaxed than I was in those early talks, I have accepted that my speaking style will never be truly 'entertaining'. I direct my energy into connecting with the audience and offering them information that is useful and practical. I still welcome feedback, of course, but I've become much better at measuring my performance against my own standards. Within seconds of wrapping up, I do a quick evaluation of my presentation by running through a mental checklist.

- Was I well prepared?
- Did I feel that I was present and focused?
- Did I stick to the agreed time frame?
- Did I include interesting anecdotes and research?
- Do I feel I made an authentic connection with the audience?
- Is there anything I'd do differently?

These questions relate to my values – my internal measuring stick – and how I answer them determines where I will put my energy next. If someone tells me that I did a fantastic job but I know that I wasn't able to connect in the way I wanted to, I might say to myself, 'That wasn't the best talk I've given,' and put extra effort into connecting next time.

In her book *Playing Big*, Tara Mohr talks about how we can unhook from praise and criticism and learn to trust our own judgement about our performance. When we do this, we become less swayed by external validation and we trust ourselves to determine what is and isn't relevant. It's also important to remember that feedback tells us less about ourselves and more about the person giving the feedback, because they're sharing what's important to them.

Experience and practice have helped me to realise that while external feedback can be valuable, I can also be the source. This creates a loop of courage where I take action, look inside for where I might have done better, and use my own instincts to decide where to go from there, and determine what my next action should be.

Measure against your own metrics

Humans have always compared themselves to others because this is one of the ways that we absorb and categorise information about the world and our place within it. When we compare our skills, appearance, behaviour or status with other members of a group, it can give us clues about how to ingratiate rather than alienate ourselves. From this point of view, comparing can be useful – but when we overuse it, it's a habit that can also rob us of joy and move our attention away from what's good in ourselves and our lives.

One of the great modern problems is that we apply comparison to the hundreds or thousands of people we see on our screens. We have windows into the lives of people in different countries and economic brackets, and more often than not, we are comparing up rather than down.

This upward comparison plays on our ego by making us feel that we aren't as beautiful/fit/wealthy/happy/charismatic as people we don't even know and will never meet. We can fall into measuring ourselves against values that aren't our own, and can easily find ourselves wanting things that don't even fit with what we genuinely want for ourselves.

This is why it's important to be mindful when spending time on social media or other online outlets, and pay attention to when this unhealthy behaviour is triggered. Unfollowing the accounts that stir up feelings of inadequacy is a good start, and so is redirecting your comparative gaze. Looking inside and measuring your own standards of success can pull you out of the comparison spiral. Here are some tips that might help.

Letting go of comparison

Tip 1: Value all that you have. Instead of focusing on what you lack, take time to reflect on what you already have. Remind yourself of your innate strengths and attributes, including the skills that come naturally to you, interests you love and anything you value in your life. Feel a sense of appreciation for your most important relationships and the role models who genuinely inspire you.

Tip 2: Compare your present self with your past self. Remember the goals and dreams you had five or ten years ago. Have you achieved or exceeded any of them? Often, we gain greater insight into the many ways we have improved our lives, skills or situations when we compare our younger selves with our older, more experienced selves, which is far more helpful than comparing ourselves with other people. Appreciate your successes, no matter how small, and feel proud of the personal obstacles you've overcome and any fears you've faced.

Tip 3. Let envy be your guide. As counterintuitive as it might seem, pay attention to the people you envy and ask yourself, *What are these feelings trying to tell me?* Very often comparisons give us a clue about what we'd like to change in our lives. If you find yourself feeling envious of someone else's career or lifestyle, reflect on the specific aspects that seem most appealing. For example, you may discover that you're not actually envious of their role or the size of their house but rather of the autonomy or flexibility their lifestyle provides.

Tip 4: Use gratitude. If you struggle to detach yourself from comparison, try bringing in gratitude. Recognise the small things you feel grateful for to help quiet your chasing ego and reconnect you to a more authentic and accepting part of yourself. I do this each day using an app called Grateful. Each evening at dinnertime, the app sounds a chime, reminding me to reflect on what went well in my day. I share these things with my husband Chris and later, save a note and sometimes a couple of photos in the app, creating a beautiful 'gratitude bank' that I can scroll through at any time to remind me of what is good in my life.

Putting yourself out there has always been scary

Given that Susan Cain wrote a bestselling book about introverts, it's not surprising to read that she hears from a lot of people who she says are 'bursting with ideas' but terrified to share them. In a 2023 newsletter about the fear of sharing new ideas, Cain wrote that this has always been the case for her, too. To illustrate how this fear affects people we might not ever suspect, she points to a phenomenon academics call 'Darwin's Delay'. It took Charles Darwin 34 years to publish his theory that humans evolved from apes, a delay scholars attribute to Darwin's fear that he would be judged for his radical concept, which went against the science and beliefs of the time.

If you find the thought of sharing your ideas, art, writing, music or designs similarly terrifying, Cain has a few useful tips:

1. You're in good company. Anyone who's ever wanted to share, lead, create or connect has had to go public with their thoughts. It has always been scary.

2. Use social media for self-expression, not self-promotion. When we use it well, social media can feel more like a creative project than self-promotion, though of course it can be both.

3. Associate idea generation with pleasure. Cain likes to work at a cosy candlelit table with chocolate at hand. Because of this, she now associates writing with pleasure.

4. Do your work in public spaces sometimes. This can be helpful even when the creative thinking process is a solo act.

5. Work at night when your cortisol levels are lower. The stress hormone cortisol peaks in the morning and falls in the evening, so though you might think clearly in the morning you are probably less inhibited at night. Creativity researchers believe that a relaxed brain is a more creative brain.

6. Strengthen your confidence in small steps. Practise asking yourself where you stand on different matters and notice everywhere you feel comfortable to stand firm on a certain decision. As Cain points out, this might be as simple as noting that you have a clear idea of how to organise your dishwasher. Savour the experience of feeling 'centred' and learn to tap in to that feeling over and again, so that you can produce ideas and make other decisions from this place.

SIXTEEN

Fear: the dreaded foe

How do you self-sabotage?

Many of the ways we undermine ourselves or 'self-sabotage' are subconscious. These behaviours often align with the characteristics Carl Jung referred to as our 'shadow' (see page 158). The shadow encompasses aspects we deny in ourselves and dislike in others, as well as those we admire in others but are hesitant to claim for ourselves. Jung's philosophy suggests that personal growth requires us to confront our shadow, embracing and reconciling all of our character traits.

Begin by observing the patterns of self-sabotage you tend to favour. Once you recognise these often unconscious thoughts and behaviours, you can begin to challenge them through your inner dialogue and your actions.

Blaming

While there may be some truth in it, blaming leaves you feeling powerless. Blaming others often accompanies a 'victim' mentality, which is disempowering. Assuming responsibility will boost your self-esteem and sense of control.

Common self-talk: 'I can't help it'; 'It's their fault'; 'Things are just really hard for me.'

Procrastination

How often do you postpone unpleasant tasks like doing your taxes, organising your space, managing your finances, starting an exercise routine, or adopting a healthier diet? Procrastination is a popular method of self-sabotage.

Common self-talk: 'I don't have the time'; 'I'm too tired'; 'The time isn't right.'

Overcommitting

Many of us overextend ourselves, saying yes to everything and ending up overwhelmed and resentful. This form of self-sabotage often distracts you from pursuing your 'real' goals, the ones that would bring you the most fulfilment if you were courageous enough to pursue them.

Common self-talk: 'They need me – I can't say no'; 'I'm the only one who will do the job well'; 'I just like to stay busy.'

Not backing yourself

This is perhaps the most widespread method of self-sabotage. It's also a self-fulfilling prophecy. The less you believe in yourself, the less likely you'll be to take on new challenges and the more likely you are to believe you are unworthy of great things (and the less possibility there is of you achieving them).

Common self-talk: 'I'm not good enough'; 'No one will want me'; 'I'm too tall, too short, too heavy, too unattractive, not interesting, or not smart enough.'

Not being prepared

We also trick ourselves into sabotaging ourselves by not being well prepared, offering ourselves an excuse for a less positive performance or the option to opt out of certain events.

Common self-talk: 'I didn't have time to prepare, which is why I didn't do well'; 'I don't have anything to wear so I won't be able to attend.'

Unclear goals or lacking direction

This is a challenging area to address as it often manifests as a pervasive sense of confusion. Not being clear about your life's desires is often tied to a fear of making wrong choices.

Common self-talk: 'I don't know what I want'; 'Nothing interests me'; 'What if I get it wrong?'

Identify your dominant self-sabotage style or styles among the above. Most people employ more than one. Start by becoming aware of your self-talk. If you're ready to challenge these thoughts, reframe them. For instance, 'I'm not good enough' could become 'I'm as capable as I need to be to give this a try.'

Then, take the next step by doing something different, for example, buy yourself one really great outfit if you're using the excuse that you don't have anything to wear or go for a ten-minute walk if you're using the excuse that you're too busy to exercise. The idea is to challenge your self-sabotage tendencies.

Trade fear for excitement

A tip I find very effective is to reframe nerves in your mind as excitement. Doing this is not only easy, it's also true, because nerves and excitement show up in the body in the same way – the only differential is mindset. Telling yourself that you are excited (a racing heart and shallow breathing can accompany a first date as readily as a presentation) and saying these words aloud allows for the emotions and feelings associated with excitement to come through, rather than those associated with fear.

The four faces of fear

Our inbuilt stress responses have kept us alive for millennia, and while they're important, our modern world triggers these responses mistakenly and this can impair function. For a long time, the two main responses were fight and flight, but in recent times two more have been added: freeze and, more recently, fawn.

When confronting a fear, it can be useful to know which type of fear response we're encountering.

Fight

When we face a threat by reacting physically in ways such as fighting back or clenching our jaws or fists, shouting, slamming doors and generally doing anything that can be categorised as aggressive. Aggression is the main characteristic. This includes:

- Crying
- Hands in fists, desire to punch

- Flexed/tight jaw, grinding teeth
- Fight in eyes, glaring, fight in voice
- Desire to stomp, kick, smash with legs, feet
- Feelings of anger/rage
- Knotted stomach/nausea, burning stomach.

Flight

This response involves running away from the threat. In the same way a deer might run from a lion, examples include literally running away from a threat, leaving a house after a fight or disagreement, not responding to people's calls or texts, ending a relationship abruptly, or avoiding commitment in a relationship. Avoidance is the main characteristic. This includes:

- Restless legs and feet or numbness in legs
- Anxiety/shallow breathing
- Big/darting eyes
- Reported or observed fidgety-ness, restlessness, feeling trapped.

Freeze

This isn't so much about movement but rather is a complete response. People who freeze often dissociate from a threat and are unable to react in the moment. They may be completely unable to respond. They might let others yell at them. They might experience a sense of dread. They might hold their breath or experience cold, numb or pale skin. Inertia is the main characteristic of freezing. This includes:

- Feeling stuck in some part of the body
- Feeling cold/frozen, numb, pale skin

- Sense of stiffness, heaviness
- Holding breath/restricted breathing
- Sense of dread, heart pounding
- Decreased heart rate (although can sometimes increase).

Fawn

This is the most recently identified stress response and is less thoroughly researched than the others. As the name suggests, fawning occurs when the person under threat tries to placate, appease or befriend their aggressor in an attempt to prevent them causing harm. This might involve people-pleasing to reduce conflict or trauma, a behaviour that often shows up in people with complex PTSD including those with childhood trauma. Fawning behaviour also includes following the lead of other people, going along with their decisions, being aware of other people's needs while ignoring your own, being overly polite or agreeable, and avoiding saying no. This includes:

- Over-apologising to others
- Difficulty saying no
- Excessively flattering the other person
- Going out of the way to please others
- Neglecting one's own needs
- Pretending to agree with others.

Most of us will likely display the same response repeatedly, and getting to know how that feels in your body can go a long way to helping you regulate that response in the moment. If you know, for example, that flight is your typical stress response, you might realise that it begins with the sensation of shaky legs. If you can consciously bring awareness to your body prior to engaging in whatever experience is triggering you, those sensations won't be as scary.

Motivate yourself by recalling moments of mastery

Career coach Nina Perry recommends boosting our confidence by reminding ourselves of our 'mastery' experiences, which are times when we've taken on a new challenge and succeeded. I invite clients to keep a record of these experiences and remind themselves of them often, and it's something I have done myself over the years.

Create a file on your computer or a folder of notes on your phone (or use a specific journal or a physical folder if you prefer) and each week, make a note of the small wins you've achieved, anything kind that has been said to you and any positive feedback you've received. If you have a regular performance review, if you're applying for a new role or even on days you need to boost your mood, this collection of moments of mastery and self-belief can be a particularly helpful resource.

Braving public speaking

We've all heard that public speaking is rated as one of life's most significant fears and many of us avoid it for that reason. But nerves around public speaking aren't limited to speaking in front of a crowd. We might feel them when we're attending a dinner party, while telling the restaurant table you're serving about the dinner specials, or at any time when all eyes are on you. The tips that follow are framed in the context of giving a formal talk, but they can also be applied to everyday situations.

Professor Sarah Gershman teaches public speaking to leaders from around the world and notes that even the most confident speakers will find ways to distance themselves from their audience without even realising it. Our brains are programmed to trigger these defensive mechanisms, so how can we overcome this?

A new and emerging area of study is proving that while our thoughts have an impact on our bodies, our bodies have an equally powerful effect on our brains. Harnessing the knowledge of how our physical actions can influence our thoughts and behaviour can be the first step to becoming a more confident and relaxed speaker.

Gershman points out that in the same way that being kind to others can help us feel physically calmer and less stressed, approaching public speaking in a similar way, with a spirit of generosity, can go a long way to counteracting the physical sensation of being under attack and therefore help us feel less nervous. She believes that it is absolutely possible to become a generous speaker no matter how nervous you may be.

Here are her three steps.

1. When preparing, think about your audience

A mistake made again and again is that people start with a focus on their speaking topic. Immediately they get lost in the detail of the presentation and this makes it harder to break down the wall between speaker and audience. When we start with the audience instead, the first question we ask is, who will be in the room? Why are they here? What are they interested in hearing? Be specific in your answers and craft a message that speaks directly to your specific audience and their specific needs.

2. Right before you speak, refocus your brain

Just as with diving off a board, leaping out of a plane, or picking up the phone to make a phone call, the moment right before you speak and take the first action is the moment you feel the most nervous. Being aware of this gives you the chance to refocus your mind.

Tap in to your purpose in this moment. If you are speaking about something you are passionate about, remind yourself why you are here and why this is worth taking a risk. Remind yourself that you are here to serve the audience. Be firm with your brain and remind it that this isn't about you, it's about your audience. After four to six presentations, your brain will start to get this message and it's likely you'll feel less nervous.

3. Make eye contact while you're speaking

It's natural to scan the room when faced with many people we don't know but when we do this, we're not really connecting with anyone, and as we know, connection makes us feel safer.

By making sustained eye contact with one person per thought, you're more likely to feel that you're just talking to one person, and this is better for introverts who prefer more focused connection. While this can feel uncomfortable at first, in genuinely connecting with several individuals, you'll be more generous in your connection with everyone.

Make fear your friend

Elizabeth Gilbert has thought a lot about fear, especially in the context of creativity – something she explores at length in her book about the nature of inspiration, *Big Magic*. Like me (and perhaps you), Liz grew up believing that fear was something to be ashamed of. And if you couldn't get rid of it, you 'should at least have the dignity to hide it'.

Stuffing fear down or pretending it doesn't exist isn't a good long-term strategy because all it succeeds in doing is creating adults who repress their real feelings and/or berate themselves for not being tougher. The shame of not being able to escape fear can multiply it exponentially.

The turning point came for Liz when she discovered that 'the opposite of fear is not courage, it's compassion. You cannot chase fear out. You can only bring love in.' When we bring love in, the fear starts to subside. Perhaps fear isn't something to be overcome, it's something to be embraced. It is just another passenger along for the ride in our minibus, as are the many other facets of our personality. Fighting with it is futile. So is trying to outmuscle it or push it out of the bus. A much better, gentler tactic is to approach it, introduce yourself, and accept it. (Some people even give their fear a name.) After all, it's simply another aspect of ourselves – imperfect, but valuable.

Like our other problematic protectors, fear exists to keep you from danger, even if it doesn't feel that way at times. You may have been told to shake off your fear and focus on living in the moment, and although these strategies can be effective in the right circumstances they don't work for everyone. They might make sense in theory, but they may not make you any less anxious when practised.

What comforted Liz was knowing she was loved, that others had experienced these same struggles with fear, and that she was seen – or as psychiatrist and author Dr Dan Siegel puts it, 'felt'. Over the years, Liz has learned to speak to herself compassionately when feeling scared. She has learned to stop whatever she's doing in those fearful moments and be alone with herself. From there, she writes herself a letter from a place she refers to as 'Love' – which is what we might call the wise or Self energy part of ourselves that we spoke about on page 145. When she's scared, nervous or daunted by the uncertainties of life, these are the words Liz writes: *I love you. I've got you. I'm not going anywhere.* And, *I'm not leaving you. I will never leave you. Whatever this is, we will face it together. You are not alone.*

Through practice, Liz has learned that what helps her most is staying with fear rather than running from it. For her, facing it head-on and holding its hand works better than any other strategy.

Facing fear with compassionate courage: Sinead's story

Like me, Sinead has her own coaching business and had a great fear of public speaking. When she first spoke to me about wanting to present a workshop on leadership, she told me she felt like a great imposter.

'I work with brilliant men and women who are learning to be better leaders and I coach them on becoming more confident speakers,' she confessed, 'but I can't face the idea myself of presenting to groups.'

Sinead and I talked about why she wanted to run workshops, and she shared a long-held dream of presenting her research project at a leadership conference one day. 'It's crazy for me to even consider being on stage in a huge auditorium, I know,' she said, 'but I genuinely care about sharing these findings with as many people as I can. I believe the world needs more compassionate and caring leaders. Imagine how much we might change organisations and our political leaders if we can convince them they can be doubly effective without being aggressive or competitive.'

Finding purpose was the first step in Sinead's journey to being a speaker. She needed to also acknowledge her strengths. We both knew her to be great at creating connections and adept at sharing a story – but because she had little experience using these strengths in a group setting, the idea of running a workshop filled her with fear.

Sinead adopted Liz's idea of allowing fear to be present. Although she felt a little odd having an internal conversation, she asked the fearful part of herself, 'What are you most afraid of?' To her amusement, it responded: 'I don't want you to make a fool of yourself or forget your words or speak in that shaky voice you sometimes have when you're nervous. Can you imagine how embarrassing that would be in front of a big group? How will they take you seriously?'

These insights were helpful for Sinead, and she started writing her fear's worries in her journal. Next, she invited a part of herself that she called 'compassionate courage' to respond. *'Maybe your voice will be shaky to begin with,'* she wrote, *'and maybe that just has to be okay. The bigger question is, how will you feel if you never take on this challenge? Don't you think you'll regret that?'*

Sinead carried on like this for some weeks and finally called to tell me she had decided to get some public speaking lessons and join her local Toastmasters. She knew that she wouldn't be the greatest speaker to begin with, but while journalling, she had an epiphany about 'growth mindset'. Sinead reflected on the fact that when she'd first taken up sailing as an adult, her early embarrassment at having very little skill or knowledge of the correct terminology was well worth the awkwardness when she eventually got the hang of it.

Like all of us when we learn something new, Sinead accepted that there was no shortcut to being a good speaker. Her only option was to take fear onto the stage for her first few performances (and if she was like many people who speak in front of large groups, maybe even every time she spoke), but she could also take her compassionate courage.

Soothe fear with loving kindness

Sit quietly with a pen and paper and write yourself a letter. Experiment with Liz's approach, and tell yourself all the things you wish someone would say to you in this moment. Think, *If the most loving, supportive and strong person in the world was here to take care of me, what would I want to hear that person say?* When the words come to mind, write them down to give yourself this gift.

If you find that this exercise does soothe your fear, consider making it a more regular part of your routine. You don't need to wait until you are in crisis mode before speaking to yourself in a kind and loving way. It can become a regular part of your day, as Liz's morning pages are, or something you do when you notice yourself feeling vulnerable or sensitive.

If the writing exercise doesn't quite do the trick, don't feel discouraged. This isn't a one-size-fits-all scenario. What works for your personality and particular type of fear might be very different. If you like the approach of building self-compassion but you're not into writing, try searching for meditations that focus on loving kindness. There are many excellent meditations on the free Insight Timer app, including one of my own.

Some people find that moving their body is the most effective way to get beyond fear. This certainly works for me. There's something about walking in nature and connecting with the vastness of the natural world that does wonders for putting my comparatively small fears into perspective.

Experiment until you find the things that work for you. When you do, build up a toolkit to help you deal with your fear – not in a combative or dominating way, but in a kind and compassionate way that acknowledges that fear is a primitive instinct doing its best to save you from unknown dangers.

Failure and growth

A person who never made a mistake never tried anything new.

Albert Einstein

Failure prevents so many people from attempting challenges where the outcome is uncertain – even when succeeding might make their lives infinitely more enjoyable or rewarding. This is especially true of introverts with perfectionist tendencies. If you're a people-pleaser who has been conditioned to be 'good', a priority for you will be reframing (conscious or subconscious) the belief that failure is something to be avoided at all costs.

This can be a challenging process, but it's well worth the effort because the freedom that comes from learning to embrace failure can be transformative. When examined objectively and with hindsight, many of our not-so-great moments come with their own successes. The Matildas' semi-final defeat to England in the 2023 FIFA Women's World Cup was a gut-wrenching loss for the players and fans of the host nation but even so, their performance was hugely successful in other ways.

By playing brilliantly on a global stage and making it all the way to the semi-finals, the Matildas cemented their place as a world-class team and brought women's football to the attention of millions of new fans. In particular, they captured the hearts of young girls, just as the players had hoped they would. They also caught the country's attention in a way no other event had. An impressive 11.15 million viewers in Australia (not to mention millions more around the world) tuned in to watch the match – the highest viewership recorded since the rating system was established in 2001. Proof that women's sport has the cachet to attract viewers, and therefore advertising dollars and sponsorship deals – investments that could well improve the working conditions and earning potential of female athletes in the future.

Failure is not a bad or shameful thing, it's a fact of life – and an inescapable one at that. A person who diligently avoids failure will still potentially fail – just not in the ways they fear. Chasing perfection in a career might come at the cost of a relationship, time with family and even your mental and physical wellbeing. Being fixated on maintaining the perfect physique might come at the expense of a full and happy social life. It's unrealistic to anticipate that you'll nail your first speaking event, be able to play a winning game of tennis or paint a beautiful landscape when you're a raw beginner, but taking the baby steps to learn could very well lead you to a meaningful outcome in the long term.

Accepting failure as a natural and essential part of life is an integral step towards personal growth, especially because our setbacks have the potential to teach us just as much as, if not more than, our wins. Think back to chapter 9, where we discussed how the events of our life shape us. It's the tough times – not the triumphs – that usually prove the most formative.

Challenge your perception of failure

How we feel about failing is determined by our mindset, so being aware of this when evaluating a failure can be a very effective way of helping us move past it – especially if we are able to reframe it as a lesson and an opportunity for growth.

Think about something that didn't go so well for you recently. Now, think carefully about how you set out to meet that challenge or situation. Try to recall all the steps you took to ensure success. It's likely you did your best, but even if you didn't, *you* are not a failure, you simply failed in this specific instance.

Can you pinpoint where things went off track? What has this experience taught you about yourself or other people? Are there any successes or silver linings hidden in this failure? You can probably identify several things you'd do differently if faced with a similar situation in the future. By identifying where things went wrong and how you might steer a different course next time, you can file this setback away as a useful lesson rather than further evidence that *you* – the person – are defective.

The beauty of failing often and fast

The road to almost any innovative product, idea or endeavour is paved with failure, so it's not surprising that the highly competitive and innovative tech world was one of the first industries to rebrand failure. Famously, Google created a company culture that encourages employees to take risks and be transparent about their failures. In 2010, Eric 'Astro' Teller – head of Google X, the company's secret laboratory – explained the company's approach to rewarding failure:

'You must reward people for failing. If not, they won't take risks and make breakthroughs. If you don't reward failure, people will hang on to a doomed idea for fear of the consequences. That wastes time and saps an organisation's spirit.'

Today, calculated risks are more likely to be seen as something to be celebrated, and even incentivised, not just at Google, but at many companies around the world that value creativity and new ideas. When judiciously applied to our own lives, this approach to failing often and failing fast can also give us confidence to try new things. Only by moving in new directions and trying new things can we introduce new energy and avoid stagnating.

SEVENTEEN

Taming imposter syndrome

The term 'imposter phenomenon' (commonly referred to as imposter syndrome) was coined by clinical psychologists Pauline Rose Clance and Suzanne Imes in the 1970s to describe the experience of feeling like a fraud. Today, 'imposter syndrome' is so ubiquitous that most people I work with are not only familiar with it, but also intimately acquainted with how it feels. Commonly, it involves the belief that we are 'fooling' others into thinking we are competent when we're not, and unfortunately, this belief often crops up even when we *are* very competent and have achievements under our belt that prove this. A poll of 750 executive women in the US revealed that as many as 75 per cent of them had experienced imposter syndrome at certain points in their career, and 85 per cent believed this was a common experience for women in corporate America.

I've experienced imposter syndrome myself and seen it in many of my clients. I've become reasonably adept at spotting it and coaching people on how to move forward in spite of it. This is crucial, because if left unchallenged, imposter syndrome has the potential to handicap us socially, professionally and creatively. It becomes another voice in our head telling us we're not worthy and preventing us from trying new things and letting our light shine.

Imposter syndrome is an equal-opportunity affliction

Possibly because imposter phenomenon was first identified in women, or maybe because it's so pervasive among women in the corporate world (perhaps in part due to a lack of representation), it's largely been seen as something that affects more women than men. This isn't the reality, though.

After talking about imposter syndrome on the TED stage in 2012, Harvard psychologist Amy Cuddy received thousands of emails from people saying they felt like a fraud – and roughly half of those emails were from men. In her book, *Presence*, Cuddy says that many, many men experience it, too.

Success doesn't appear to be the antidote to imposter syndrome we might assume, and in some cases, it can make things worse because it only adds to that sense of internal pressure.

When Mike Cannon-Brookes finished university and started a company with his friend, Scott Farquar, one of their motivations was avoiding a conventional job. Over the next 15 years, Mike's imposter syndrome grew in line with his company. As Atlassian grew from a two-man start-up to a multi-billion-dollar business, so did Mike's fear of being 'found out'. In board meetings, Mike would scribble down the acronyms being thrown around so he could look them up online later. He recalls that he felt 'like a five-year-old' who was way out of his depth.

When Atlassian was selected to represent Australia at the World Entrepreneur of the Year Awards in Monte Carlo, Mike found himself seated next to the winner from Portugal – a 65-year-old man who'd spent 35 years running a company with a turnover of €4 billion and 30,000 employees. After talking for a while, Mike confessed to feeling like an imposter in this crowd. He even joked that he and Scott would be sent back to Australia once somebody figured them out.

To his surprise, his Portuguese neighbour said he felt exactly the same way, and added that he suspected all of the other winners in that room did, too. This was a light bulb moment for the young founder. Imposter syndrome was clearly something that everybody deals with to at least some extent, regardless of how successful they are.

What we know is that imposter syndrome is most likely to strike when someone is stretching themselves in *any* way and in *any* field. It might show up when you achieve something you've long been working towards, when you're offered an incredible opportunity or any time you feel remotely out of your depth. Imposter syndrome whispers that your success is a result of 'luck' and not earned, and that it's only a matter of time before everyone discovers what you already know to be true: you're a fraud and this house of cards is on the verge of collapse. Being highly qualified and good at your job doesn't make you immune.

Learn to use your imposter syndrome to your advantage

Mike's experience at that awards dinner showed him that he could continue moving forward in life regardless of his challenging and persistent feelings of imposter syndrome, especially if he could learn to harness them in a positive way.

Accepting that imposter syndrome was part and parcel of being out of his depth in some way was his first step. Instead of seeing it as a bad thing and looking for ways to 'conquer' it, he simply became more aware of when imposter syndrome was influencing his emotions and behaviours.

In his TED Talk on imposter syndrome, Mike observed that the most successful people he knows don't question *themselves*, they question their *knowledge*. When their imposter syndrome flares up, they recognise that it's because they might be in over their heads. Rather than run from the challenge or ignore that voice, he recommends taking it as a cue to ask for advice, gather new information or test your ideas. The result of this is that you might be better prepared for a challenge, having learned what you needed to. As Mike points out, it's okay to be out of your depth so long as you don't freeze.

Seek connection

By sharing his vulnerable feelings with the man seated next to him, Mike tapped into one of the most effective ways to overcome imposter syndrome: connecting with others. This is a tactic that nearly three-quarters of the executive women who reported feeling imposter syndrome also said they employ. If they find themselves doubting their ability to take on a new role, they look to a mentor or advisor for guidance and reassurance. Women also pointed to having a supportive manager and feeling valued as two other factors that helped them to combat imposter syndrome.

When used in this way, connection can be an antidote to these anxieties, especially when we share our vulnerabilities and give others permission to express theirs. When we remember that most of the people around us are likely feeling the same way, we are better able to look at ourselves more compassionately and treat ourselves with greater kindness.

Focus on another person's comfort to ease your discomfort

Our brains are not good at multitasking, and this can work to our advantage when we shift our focus from our feelings of inadequacy to making the people around us feel more at ease. If you feel uncomfortable in a room or situation, it's highly likely that the other people who are with you do too.

Look for clues in their body language. Is anyone avoiding eye contact, lowering their head, speaking quietly or withdrawing into themselves? These are often signs that someone feels out of their element. Consider how you might be able to help that person feel more at ease. If they are a stranger, can you say hello and introduce yourself? If they're a colleague or acquaintance, inviting them to sit next to you might be the tiny lifeline they need in this moment. If you're the leader, consider how you can make room for everyone to feel welcome and able to speak up. Is there something you can do to break the ice or let the people around you know they aren't alone? If you're running a meeting, could you ask the people who didn't get much airtime if they'd like to be added to the agenda next time? Some people find it easier to contribute when given the space to express themselves without interruption.

Tap in to your *why*

Cortnee Vine, a winger for the Sydney Football Club, joined the Matildas during their campaign for the Asian Cup in 2022. In an interview with the *Sydney Morning Herald* ahead of the Women's 2023 World Cup, she confessed that joining the national team had ignited feelings of imposter syndrome and made her question if she belonged on the squad. Being selected had also added more pressure to perform for Sydney FC, as she felt she should always 'be killing it' now that she was a Matilda.

Vine has developed a few strategies to deal with this increased pressure. One of these is a tattoo on her right middle finger, a Viking symbol that means 'create your reality'. She has a similar motto on display in her bedroom to keep her grounded in this mindset.

If she finds herself questioning why she is putting herself through these experiences, she strips everything back to its simplest form and returns to *why* she plays: because she loves it. Her love for the game is the thing that gives her the courage to keep moving. Another *why* that motivates Vine is her desire to show young Australian girls that a footballing career is a possibility for them: 'If we can encourage young girls to get into football by how we play at this World Cup. That's what I want out of it.'

Harnessing a 'why' for courageous action:
Gemma's story

Recently, an acquaintance of mine, Gemma, shared a story that perfectly illustrates the power of a meaningful 'why' when facing imposter syndrome. Gemma is married, has two dogs, a big family, and an active social life. For fifteen years, she's built a reputation as one of the best hair colourists in the country, but after years of working fulltime and travelling for her work, she scaled back to make room for other interests. Now, she travels frequently, plays recreational sports and paints for her own enjoyment. A few times a week, she volunteers at a local dog rescue centre – something she's enormously passionate about.

When a friend suggested they take a girls' holiday to the Philippines, Gemma saw an opportunity to link this trip with her love of dogs. She'd been following the Instagram account of Dumaguete Animal Sanctuary (DAS), a rescue centre based in the Philippines. On a whim, Gemma decided to message them and ask if she could visit while in the country. She'd never done anything like this before, and had no idea if they would reply or agree, but to her surprise, they invited her to take a tour of their facility.

Several months out from the trip, while organising canvases she'd painted at home, Gemma had an idea that was also completely out of character for her: *If I could sell a few of these paintings*, she thought, *I might be able to raise some money for DAS.* As an amateur artist with no formal training, Gemma painted purely for her own enjoyment. She'd only ever shared her work with friends or family who'd happened to wander into her kitchen while she was painting. She hated being the centre of attention, so the thought of strangers and even people she knew looking at her paintings made her uncomfortable, but she couldn't let go of the idea. Volunteering at the local rescue centre had taught her that every donation – no matter how small – was vital to keeping the doors open.

Swallowing her nerves, she asked the owner of the salon where she worked if she might be able to hold an art show there. Her boss was more than happy to let her use the space, and the event was officially in motion. A date was set and Gemma started telling people about it in person and on social media. This was another terrifying step because it took her art show from being an idea to something real. When I commented on how courageous it was for her to put herself out there like this, Gemma said: 'I was so nervous that nobody would come, or that people would come and I wouldn't sell anything, but I decided that it was worth the potential embarrassment.'

When the designated Friday evening finally arrived, Gemma's co-workers helped her set up trays of drinks and nibbles, and carried in nearly 50 pieces that she'd painted over the past few years. After arranging them around the room and pricing them to sell, they turned up the music and waited. Within the hour, the salon was full of people taking in Gemma's work and asking her about the rescue centre. By the end of the evening, every single painting had sold, and she'd raised an incredible $5000 for DAS – money she was able to give them in person when she and her friend visited Dumaguete. Gemma and her friend were given a tour of the rescue centre and spent several hours getting to know the staff and the more than 17. dogs in their care.

Courage and vulnerability were the two things that enabled Gemma to have this wonderful experience and share this incredible gift. Through a series of small actions, she set a chain of events in motion and pushed herself well beyond her comfort zone. Each one of these steps took courage: messaging the rescue centre, asking her boss to use the salon, posting about the event on Facebook and Instagram, and showing up on the night, determined to see her commitment through regardless of the outcome. Gemma's desire to make a difference in the lives of suffering animals fuelled every one of these actions. Like Cortnee Vine, the strength of her *why* outmuscled her sense of imposter syndrome.

Tips for bypassing imposter syndrome

Just as we might never be entirely free of our shadow self or inner critic, imposter syndrome will continue to rear its head. This is why our objective isn't to conquer or eliminate it entirely but to accept its presence in our lives and see it as simply another companion on the road to growth. From there, we can become skilled at detouring around it. To that end, here are some tips you may find useful the next time it makes an appearance.

1. Recognise that it's common

Understand that imposter syndrome is a common experience that affects many high-achieving individuals. Remind yourself that you are not alone in feeling this way.

2. Identify your strengths and accomplishments

Take time to acknowledge and appreciate your achievements. Make a list of your skills, talents and accomplishments to remind yourself of your capabilities.

3. Challenge your negative self-talk

Pay attention to your negative self-talk and self-doubt. Replace self-critical thoughts with positive and affirming statements. Focus on your strengths and remind yourself of past successes.

4. Embrace a 'growth mindset'

Shift your perspective from a focus on perfection to one of continuous learning and growth. Embrace challenges as opportunities for growth and view setbacks as valuable learning experiences.

5. Seek support

Reach out to supportive friends, mentors or colleagues who can provide encouragement and perspective. Share your feelings of self-doubt and seek their feedback and support.

6. Normalise (and maybe even celebrate) failure

Accept that making mistakes and experiencing setbacks is a normal part of the learning process. Reframe failure as a stepping stone to success and an opportunity for growth.

7. Keep a success journal

Create a journal to document your achievements, positive feedback and moments of success. Reviewing this journal during moments of self-doubt can help counteract imposter syndrome.

8. Celebrate progress

Recognise and celebrate your progress, no matter how small. Acknowledge and reward yourself for stepping outside your comfort zone and taking on new challenges.

9. Practise self-compassion

Treat yourself with kindness and compassion. Be understanding and forgiving of your mistakes and imperfections, just as you would be towards a friend.

10. Embrace the discomfort

Accept that feeling uncomfortable or uncertain is a natural part of growth. Embrace the discomfort as a sign that you are stretching yourself and making progress.

Courage summary

- Courage isn't the absence of fear but the ability to be brave, even when fear is present.
- Being vulnerable, being willing to have open and difficult conversations and boundary setting are acts of courage that can boost your confidence.
- The recipe for courage is:
  Action + feedback + self-reflection = courage
- Avoid comparison as you build courage.
- Make fear your friend as you work towards building courage (and embrace compassion when you're fearful).
- Tackle imposter syndrome by reminding yourself that it's common, reconnect with your strengths, challenge your negative self-talk, embrace a 'growth mindset', find some support, and normalise your mistakes and missteps.

Part Four

Presence

'There is a middle path but it goes only one direction: toward the light. Your light. The one that goes *blink, blink, blink* inside your chest when you know what you're doing is right. Listen to it. Trust it. Let it make you stronger than you are.'

Cheryl Strayed, *Tiny Beautiful Things*

When we bring together all of the concepts introduced earlier, we begin to focus less on the opinions of others and more on what is truly right for us. We align our lives with our chosen values, engage our unique strengths and embrace the part of us that knows how to be courageous. We turn towards what we might think of as our own inner light, the deep part of ourselves that is wise, intuitive and grounded. It is in this place that we might also access our capacity for 'presence'.

EIGHTEEN

The power of presence

When someone is described as having 'presence', it usually means they are attuned to whatever is happening in the moment and not focusing on past events, future worries or current anxieties. They are deeply engaged with whatever is going on. It's a state where they are free from distractions, fully attentive, and immersed in their current activity or interaction. This engagement with the moment is called 'being present', and though it's not the same thing as presence, the two are closely related.

Aspiring to develop presence within ourselves encourages us to tap in to the calm, centred energy within. Doing this brings immediate self-awareness and gives us a chance to choose how we respond and behave. The act of striving towards presence ensures that we will become better at living in the present moment, which is a place where we can make more mindful choices about the person we want to be.

Having presence requires that a person be living authentically, communicating openly and engaging with the here and now. Perhaps this is why people said to have presence seem to naturally command respect and confidence. We sense that they trust themselves, which boosts our trust in them, too. When a person conducts themselves with dignity during challenging situations, demonstrates emotional intelligence, and is viewed by others as being someone who remains calm under pressure, they can be said to 'have presence'. Listening actively, articulating ideas clearly, and being persuasive when it's called for are other traits of this quality.

You probably know someone who you'd describe as having this kind of presence and it's likely you'd agree that it's impactful. Clients who work for leaders like this describe them as having gravitas and charisma – they are people who command a great degree of confidence and respect. They're people who make you feel seen, heard, valued and acknowledged, and it's often said that when you're in the company of someone like this, they make you feel that you're the only person in the room.

Executive (and non-executive) presence

A 2018 study of corporate leaders found that while hard work, performance and sponsors help talented people to get recognised and promoted in the workplace, the factor that makes the biggest difference to advancement is what they call 'executive presence'. This key finding is significant because it reveals that when evaluating candidates for a promotion, leaders are likely to place more value on an intangible quality – the *je ne sais quoi* of presence – than on tangible attributes that can be measured and quantified, such as certain skillsets or performance. Perhaps this comes back to trust: candidates with executive presence trust themselves, and their leaders pick up on that energy and reward it with professional advancement.

This same study outlined three pillars of executive presence and the key attributes for each pillar.

The three pillars of executive presence

1. Gravitas

- Exudes confidence and grace under fire
- Acts decisively
- Shows integrity and 'speaks truth to power'
- Demonstrates emotional intelligence
- Burnishes their reputation
- Projects vision

2. Communication

- Great speaking skills
- Has the ability to command a room
- Demonstrates the ability to read an audience

3. Grooming and attractiveness

- Though only 5 per cent of the leaders surveyed considered appearance a key factor in executive presence, being well groomed still has the potential to impact how we are perceived

Finding gravitas: Monique's story

When Monique came to see me, she said that she wanted to achieve more 'gravitas'. Working in a competitive top-tier law firm, with a view to becoming a partner, she knew that it was critical that she portray an image of quiet confidence and dignity in order to command more respect. Her natural emotional intelligence worked in her favour, but Monique's introverted nature meant she was often overlooked as a figure of authority within her workplace. We worked together to consider how she could command more presence.

Monique began by making herself more visible across her organisation. Her first step was to speak to her partner about starting a 'women in leadership' group to mentor and support female lawyers. In addition to this, and despite her fear of public speaking, she offered to present a paper at the partner's quarterly forum later in the year. In preparation, she set herself a mini challenge to speak up more often in meetings.

Over the coming months, Monique's days were incredibly busy. The leadership group was well received and the research she was undertaking for the partner's forum gained interest from a few senior colleagues. With these new development areas to focus on as well as her already full workload, Monique discovered an interesting by-product to these changes. With less time to ruminate, she found herself having to make decisions more quickly. This created a powerful shift for Monique and she started to see herself differently.

As her profile grew, she became aware that others in the workplace were taking her more seriously. Coupled with a few small changes in her body language, Monique felt sure she was gaining more gravitas.

Dress confidently for the life you have

The third pillar is an interesting one because how attractive we are is not only subjective, it's largely beyond our control. Being well groomed, however, is something we can achieve with a little effort and know-how. Feeling good about how we present ourselves can have a big impact on our confidence and influence the way other people interact with us. This is an area sometimes overlooked by introverts – because of our desire to stay hidden, we don't want to be overly showy with our style.

When I interviewed Lisa Stockman, a personal stylist in Melbourne, we discussed the power of what we wear and the importance of finding a style that reflects our true personality. Lisa says that when most of us look in a mirror, our eyes automatically go to the aspects of our appearance we don't like. However, these are never the things she notices when meeting people. 'It might be that I see someone for the first time and think, *She has the most amazing hair* or *She has beautiful eyes that sparkle. Wow, she has a fabulous neckline.* I'm thinking of all the things I can highlight.' This is something we can do for ourselves too.

For many people, working with a stylist can be a vulnerable experience; old clothes aren't 'just clothes', they are reminders of the person we were years or even decades earlier. They represent sizes we may never be again or moments of youthful freedom we can't recapture. Letting go of those versions of ourselves can be difficult, but it's often necessary if we want to convey ourselves in a way that feels empowering, authentic and current.

Your own sense of style: Carmela's story

A few years after having her children, Carmela decided to work with a stylist to help improve the way she felt about her appearance. Like most women, her body had changed since having children and she had lost confidence in her ability to choose clothes that were flattering and reflective of the person she wanted to portray.

Her recent habit had been to rush through the experience of shopping, buying things she didn't truly love or letting retail assistants talk her into items that weren't really right. As well as the desire to have someone help her find her own sense of style, Carmela made the decision to invest in a stylist in order to spend more wisely on fashion.

Despite embarrassment at the state of her wardrobe and the haphazard blend of clothing, Carmela invited her stylist Sue to her home and together, they went through every item. Sue reassured Carmela that every one of her clients felt the same way about the state of their wardrobes and clothing choices.

After Carmela tried on each item and put together different combinations, Sue was able to help her find a couple of outfits that felt like the real her – classic, stylish combinations that focused on the areas of her body to highlight. To Carmela's surprise, Sue's shopping list was brief and even before adding any new items to her wardrobe, she now had a sense of how to dress to portray greater confidence.

Connect with your personal style

If styling isn't a skill that comes naturally to you, try the following tips from Lisa to help you build an effective and impactful personal style that reflects who you are and what you want the world to know about you.

1. Write down three words that describe how you want to *feel* in your clothes in different settings. E.g., comfortable, sophisticated, at ease. The words you choose will depend on where you're going and what you'll be doing.

2. Next, write down three words that describe what you want to *project* to the world. E.g., confident, classic, creative. One of the things Lisa wants to project is *style*, because she's representing her business wherever she goes. This doesn't mean wearing a glamorous dress to the supermarket, but it does mean being intentional about the outfits she puts together.

3. Finally, write down all of the things you do in a week, and shop for the life you are living. Spending hundreds of dollars on a dress you'll only wear to one event isn't a good use of funds if you don't own a work outfit you feel great in. Invest in core basics that can be mixed and matched (e.g., classic pants, jeans, a white blouse, a trench coat, a well-cut suit or a little black dress). If you're unsure about where to begin, Google 'capsule wardrobe' and discover how to put together the basics.

Body language

In her book *Presence*, Amy Cuddy describes true presence as having an internalised sense of control and efficacy. She believes that when we develop a strong sense of presence, we're more likely to command the respect of others and we're inclined to speak with poise and clarity. We're more likeable to others and likely to feel good about ourselves. On a personal level, presence helps us feel more powerful and in turn, boosts our resilience and confidence, making us less vulnerable to the negative effects of stress.

Being attuned to and able to express our authentic thoughts, feelings, values and potential are some of the factors that play a role in whether a person has presence. A strong connection with ourselves makes us more open, optimistic and willing to take risks. It also makes us more inclined to recognise opportunities and seize them when they come our way.

The opposite is true when we feel we lack presence, which is accompanied by a sense of powerlessness, leading to increased self-focus. Becoming more aware of the mental noise generated by self-doubt and fear of judgement makes being genuinely present easier, and therefore increases the likelihood of embodying presence.

This points to a strong mind–body connection in our experience of presence. While we've long known that body language plays a huge role in the messages we give and receive, exactly how big an effect this has is widely debated. Because body language is subtle and varied and much of it is unconscious, the study of it is not an exact science. However, what is certain is that it's confusing for people if our body is sending a message that contradicts our words. For example, if you say, 'I'm having a great time' but your tone is flat and you are physically tense and fidgety, it's likely that the person you're talking to won't trust that what you're telling them is true.

The way we carry ourselves doesn't just communicate messages to *other people*, it also communicates messages to *ourselves*. Therefore, our own body language impacts our confidence. Physical poses and postures such as the 'power poses' Cuddy began adopting in her own bid to build confidence can potentially influence our psychological state, either reinforcing or transforming our feelings and self-perceptions.

Most of us resort to certain physical habits when we're uneasy, like fidgeting with our clothing or repeatedly touching our face or hair, and these behaviours can make us look and feel less confident. Experts in body language call these habits 'adaptors' because they help us to deal with the discomfort of certain situations or feelings. These habits are all done unconsciously and in response to a feeling such as stress, anxiety or worry.

It's useful to notice which adaptors you fall back on in moments of discomfort because they form a big part of the messages you're sending. If you find yourself fidgeting, tapping your pen, fiddling with your glasses, folding your arms or slumping in your chair, try sending positive non-verbal cues instead, such as maintaining eye contact, having a firm handshake and demonstrating an attentive posture. These small changes can help relax you and convey greater presence.

Putting effort into eliminating filler words like 'um' and 'ah' from your speech is another great way to improve the message you're sending, as these words make us sound unsure of ourselves. Women frequently undermine themselves by habitually including words in their written and verbal communication that make them come across as less competent and less confident. Some of these include the overuse of the following:

1. **Just** – 'I was just wondering' or 'I just want to check.'
2. **Actually** – 'I actually think . . .' or 'Actually, I'd like to add something.'
3. **Qualifiers** – 'I may not be an expert in this area' or 'I haven't done all of the research.'

4. A little bit – 'I'll just take a moment of your time' or 'I'd like to tell you a little bit about a new product.'

5. Making statements that sound like questions by raising your voice at the end of a statement.

Women are often in the habit of apologising too often and unnecessarily. Speaking experts also highlight the importance of not being overly verbose, not speaking too quickly and avoiding a monotone voice.

Training yourself to be more aware of your language and your communication style means you'll use undermining words and phrases less frequently. Learning to communicate articulately and succinctly is something all of us can practise, but it can take time to break our old habits. Awareness, focus and possibly even professional speaking training can help you feel more empowered and engaging.

Build your gravitas

While many believe gravitas is an innate quality that is less available to introverts, it is something that everyone can build. In the same way Monique did, start by setting yourself a few small challenges to build your presence in the workplace.

- Remember that many introverts have an outwardly calm composure, which can immediately put others at ease. Build on this through the mindfulness practices listed on pages 266–7.
- Portray greater confidence through your body language. Make eye contact more often, deepen your breathing as you move your body into a confident, upright (but not rigid) posture, and use words that portray greater confidence.

- Raise your profile in the workplace by offering to take on a project that will increase your visibility.
- Proactively build supportive relationships. Informal networking is an excellent way to build your visibility. Arrive a few minutes early at meetings to give you time to interact informally, reach out to someone senior in your organisation to ask if they have time for coffee so you can learn a little about their career path. Make a regular commitment to reach out to someone outside your organisation to build your informal network.

NINETEEN

Coming back to the present moment

Many introverts have the superpower of portraying a sense of calm. While you may not always feel this way on the inside, your natural inclination for reflection and your desire for 'quiet' over being overly stimulated, create a wonderful foundation for presence. You can build on this with regular practice.

Being fully engaged and grounded in the moment is a hallmark of presence, and the first step towards cultivating this is practising mindfulness, since this increases our capacity for self-awareness.

Practices such as meditation, mindful movement, breathwork, centring and grounding can help to cultivate mindful awareness. Engaging in one or several of these practices on a regular basis (when not in a state of stress) will lay a solid foundation that you can call on during more challenging moments.

Mindfulness meditation

Mindfulness meditation involves focusing on the present moment in a non-judgemental manner. It's about observing your breath, senses, bodily sensations, thoughts and feelings without getting overly caught up in them. Rather than dwelling on the past or worrying about the future, mindfulness meditation teaches us how to be fully engaged with the here and now. Here are the instructions I share with clients who are new to meditation to get them started.

Find a quiet space: Begin by finding a quiet place where you won't be disturbed. This might be your living room or bedroom, your car or your office, a spot in your local park or a dedicated meditation space if you have one.

Choose a comfortable position: While a handful of people choose to sit cross-legged on a floor cushion, most people find practising in a chair more comfortable. The key is to maintain a posture where you can be both relaxed and alert.

Set a time limit: Set a time limit, such as five or ten minutes. The free meditation app Insight Timer includes a meditation timer option that will sound a bell at the completion of your practice. Over time, as you become more accustomed to the practice, you can gradually increase the duration.

Focus on your breath: Take a few deep breaths to centre yourself. Then let your breath return to its natural rhythm. Pay attention to the sensation of the breath as it enters and leaves your nostrils and the way it creates movement in your chest and abdomen.

Observe without judgement: As you focus on your breath, you'll inevitably notice that your mind begins to wander. This is entirely natural. When this happens, gently acknowledge the thoughts or distractions and guide your attention back to your breath. The key is not to judge or chastise yourself but to simply observe the experience of breathing.

Expand your awareness: Once you become comfortable with focusing on your breath, begin to expand your awareness to other sensations. This might include the sounds around you, the feeling of the floor or chair beneath you, or the sensations in your hands and feet.

Incorporate mindfulness into everyday life

While setting aside dedicated time for meditation is beneficial, mindfulness can also be practised at any moment.

Eating: Focus on the taste, texture and smell of your food.

Walking: Notice the sensation of your feet touching the ground.

Listening: When someone is speaking to you, engage with what they are saying without formulating a response in your head.

Waiting: Instead of reaching for your phone when in a queue, take the opportunity to observe and be present in your surroundings.

Whenever mindfulness occurs to you: Tune in to the sights and sounds around you whenever you want to be present. A simple way to do this is to mentally name everything you can see, smell, hear, feel and taste. The blue of the sky, the rustling of leaves, the crunch of gravel under your feet, the cool air on your face.

Mindful movement

Mindful movement is a way of embodying presence, anchoring our awareness to the sensation of our bodies. It includes any kind of movement that brings full awareness to our physical actions, merging the mind and body. The following practices help to cultivate a greater mind–body connection.

Yoga: This ancient practice is perhaps the most well-known form of mindful movement, emphasising breathing, posture and awareness.

Tai chi: Often described as 'meditation in motion', tai chi involves a series of slow, deliberate movements accompanied by deep breathing.

Qigong: This traditional Chinese practice is often considered a more accessible form of tai chi. It blends gentle movement, meditation and breath regulation to enhance the flow of energy in the body.

Walking meditation: Rather than walking for exercise or to get from one place to another, walking meditation involves walking slowly and deliberately, focusing fully on the sensation of each step and being more aware of your environment.

Dance: All forms of dance can be mindful movement if we're fully present to our experience. Dance can help us build presence if we allow ourselves to be expansive in our movement, attuned to our physical presence and genuinely connected with the music.

Breathwork: Breathwork refers to any breathing technique where we deliberately focus on the act of breathing. Ancient Eastern medicinal traditions such as Ayurveda and traditional Chinese medicine have used these breathing practices for thousands of years to soothe the body and mind. Even just a few minutes of breathwork can help restore relaxation to the body, particularly during or after a period of stress. Choose one of the following methods and practise it for a few minutes each day.

1. Diaphragmatic breathing (or belly breathing)

- If you're new to this practice, it's easiest done initially lying on your back.
- Place one hand on your chest and the other on your abdomen.
- Breathe in deeply through your nose, ensuring that your diaphragm is expanding rather than your chest. Your abdomen will rise.
- Exhale slowly through your mouth or nose, letting your abdomen fall.
- Continue this pattern for several minutes, focusing on the rise and fall of your abdomen.

2. 4-7-8 breathing

- Inhale slowly through your nose for a count of four.
- Hold your breath for a count of seven.
- Exhale completely through your mouth for a count of eight.
- This completes one cycle. Repeat the cycle three more times.

3. Box breathing

- Inhale through your nose for a count of four.
- Hold your breath for a count of four.
- Exhale through your mouth for a count of four.
- Pause and hold your breath for another count of four.
- Repeat the process.

Centring: Centring is an exercise derived from the ancient traditions of yoga and martial arts. In many Eastern philosophies, it is believed that the source of our energy – *ki* in Japanese and *qi* in Chinese – is located in our torso, approximately two finger-widths below the navel and halfway between our belly and spine. This point is commonly referred to as our centre of gravity (hence the term 'centred').

When connected to this source of energy, we are more balanced emotionally and physically more stable, not to mention remarkably stronger. Many great athletes, artists and professionals in all fields are centred when performing at their best. Regularly practising centring has many benefits including helping with focus and concentration, alleviating anxiety and fear, keeping us calm during conflict, lowering stress levels and connecting us to a vital part of ourselves while grounding us in a way that allows us to be authentically ourselves. Like most new practices, centring may take time to master, but the benefits it offers are endless.

Centring exercise
- In a standing position, focus your attention on your centre of gravity.
- Look straight ahead and let your eyes soften.
- Let your body relax, making sure your knees aren't locked, and breathe comfortably.
- Once your physical body is centred, pay attention to the feeling of greater mental clarity.
- Imagine you can draw on and project the feeling of being centred into your voice, your gaze and all of the activities you're about to engage in.

- The 'hidden messages' in this technique are that you don't have to be tense to be strong and that you are able to create a subtle shift in your mental state through physically centring.

Grounding: Grounding involves coming into direct contact with the earth. Walking barefoot on grass, sand or soil (also known as 'earthing') or lying on these surfaces can be grounding, as can sitting with your back against a tree. Engaging with the earth by gardening, planting or even just digging in the soil can also be grounding.

The theory behind this practice is that connecting to the electrical charge being emitted by the earth can help to stabilise the electrical environment inside our body. In recent decades, several scientific studies have explored the potential health benefits of grounding. These studies have been small in scale but suggest that grounding can reduce inflammation, improve sleep and reduce stress. It is also believed to increase energy and have a positive effect on mood.

While these results are promising, this is still a relatively young theory. More rigorous research on a larger scale is needed to fully validate the health benefits of grounding. However, given that grounding is a relatively low-risk activity with many potential benefits, there's no harm in trying some of these techniques to see if they work for you. My own experience tells me that they can be enormously helpful in reconnecting us to the present moment and allowing us to draw calming energy from our physical surroundings. In addition to the earthing techniques mentioned above, try the following exercise.

Physical grounding: The 5-4-3-2-1 technique

- Identify five things you can see around you.
- Identify four things you can touch.
- Identify three things you can hear.
- Identify two things you can smell.
- Identify one thing you can taste.

Using these tools in the moment

Next time you're in a social setting or a meeting where you feel nervous because all eyes are on you, call on these tools to guide you back to the present moment. These steps can be completed in under one minute.

- Use one of the breathing methods to bring your awareness back into your body.
- Let yourself feel grounded and present by drawing your attention to your feet on the floor, your legs and back against the chair.
- Shift your posture slightly, lifting from the top of your head and aligning your body to its centre.
- Imagine you can draw on the energy at your centre and project this energy through your presence.

Once we develop a greater capacity for being in the moment, presence can be elevated through activities that connect us with something bigger than ourselves. Embracing awe, finding solace in nature and discovering spirituality are the next areas to explore.

TWENTY

Connecting with something bigger than ourselves

Our quest for presence can be bolstered by expanding our awareness outside ourselves. Spirituality and connecting to nature have the capacity to unite us with something far larger and more significant than our individual existence. This feeling, of marvelling at our smallness in the face of a vast and unknowable universe, is often described as 'awe', and it can be experienced in many ways. The depths of human compassion, the beauty of nature and the transcendence we feel when connecting to these things can evoke a profound sense of humility and wonder. These experiences remind us that there is a world out there that is often beyond our comprehension, offering a valuable and wider sense of perspective.

Throughout human history, nature has been a powerful source of awe and a symbol of life's interconnectedness. Nature reminds us that we are not as separate and singular as we might feel, and in fact, we are a small part of an intricate and mysterious web that encompasses all living things.

Spirituality is often intertwined with awe because it provides a framework for seeking a deeper understanding of this connection and offers rituals and practices that facilitate a sense of oneness with a higher power or a universal consciousness. Like nature, spirituality serves as a reminder that our lives are intertwined with a reality that transcends the boundaries of our individuality, fostering a sense of unity and purpose that is bigger than ourselves.

Embracing the science of awe

The emotion of awe is the profound feeling we experience when confronted with something vast, transcendent or unimaginably beautiful.

Awe does more than just give us goosebumps; it can change our understanding of the world and even improve our sense of wellbeing. It's an emotion that both humbles and elevates. Whether we experience it through gazing at a starry sky, listening to a soul-stirring piece of music or being moved by a small act of kindness, awe reminds us of the beauty and mystery of life.

One study also found that awe helps us to recognise 'the vastness and complexity of the world', giving us a greater sense of perspective about our own small place in the grand scheme of things. It can help us to focus less on the default self (i.e., the part of us that emphasises how we are distinct from others), which is enormously beneficial because being overly focused on this aspect of self is what gives rise to our feelings of anxiety, rumination, depression and self-criticism. Awe can increase our feelings of connectedness, boosting our mood, and even minimising materialism.

Although it is often perceived as a deeply personal experience, research suggests that awe also influences our social behaviours, particularly with regard to our capacity for kindness and generosity. In one study, participants who recalled an awe-inspiring moment showed a higher inclination to volunteer or assist a charity compared to those who reminisced about a happy moment. Researchers believed that recalling awe made participants feel as if they had more time available, leading them to be more open to offering their time for others. Individuals reflecting on awe-filled experiences felt less rushed and impatient than those recalling a joyous memory.

Intense experiences of awe can create life-impacting changes in how we perceive ourselves and the world. I had my own profound experience of this over a decade ago when I was invited to travel to Darwin to work on a project with Tourism NT. On an unseasonably sunny afternoon at the end of the wet season, my guide Ingrid Sanders took me to visit Ubirr, an ancient Indigenous art site in Kakadu National Park.

The rock artworks, depicting traditional Indigenous creation stories, were magnificent and had been beautifully protected and cared for. Combined with the subsequent view from the top of the rocky plateau, the entire experience was awe-inspiring.

From the lookout, we had a 360-degree view of the national park. Directly below, the lush green Nadab Floodplain stretched as far as the eye could see. In the distance, the sea of green looked devoid of texture as it made way for the snaking shape of the East

Alligator River. To the northeast, we could see the rocky escarpment that borders Arnhem Land and behind us were the rugged shapes of the stone country.

For a day so sunny and clear, it was surprising that we were the only people there – something that Ingrid told me was virtually unheard of. In the late-afternoon light, an eagle made a slow and methodical circle above the floodplain and in that moment, the entire world felt silent, expansive and still.

In this immense wilderness, which has been inhabited by Indigenous people for over 60,000 years, I became aware of my own insignificance. I felt a great sense of perspective and the recognition that many of my small worries and anxieties are irrelevant in the grand scheme of things.

Places of natural beauty can fill us with awe and inspiration, but they can also provide a sanctuary that helps us view our problems differently. There's nothing like standing under a big sky to remind you that there are greater forces at work. Tapping in to this calm and uplifting energy can remind you of your own well of energy within.

Embracing the eight wonders of life

Through his research, author Dacher Keltner identified what he calls the 'eight wonders of life' – easily accessible practices and experiences that we can embrace in order to weave more awe into our everyday lives.

1. Moral beauty

Keltner says other people are most likely to bring us into contact with what he calls 'everyday awe'. We find it in the actions of our workmates, family members, friends and even strangers when we witness acts of courage, kindness, strength and overcoming. The long-held view is that we find our moral compass in 'the study of great texts, or the leadership of charismatic gurus and great sages'. But we're just as likely to find what he calls 'our moral law within' when we witness the inspiring behaviour of the people around us.

2. Collective effervescence

This term is borrowed from Émile Durkheim, a French sociologist who explored the emotion at the core of religion. People commonly experience collective effervescence at events such as weddings, christenings, graduations and funerals. Everyday occurrences of collective effervescence can be experienced when we are moving in unison: walking or running with others, cheering for our team at a sporting event or marching in a protest.

3. Nature

One of the most accessible sources of awe is nature (or what Keltner also calls 'wild awe'). We find awe in the power of the ocean, the majesty of a mountain range or while walking under towering trees. Nature's more dramatic events provide us with a different kind of awe – thunderstorms, lightning, wildfires and earthquakes. Known as 'threat-based awe', this negative variant is thought to strengthen social ties among community members.

4. Music

Awe has the power to truly transport people, and Keltner writes that music 'stirs awe by opening our bodies to its neurophysiological profile'. In a study of people from 26 cultures, people shared that music had the capacity to bring 'moments of clarity, of epiphany, of truth, of really knowing their place in the great scheme of life'. We experience this kind of awe when we play music together, when we listen collectively at a concert, when we engage with music alone and when we sing or chant in a group.

5. Visual design

We also experience awe through what Keltner calls 'sacred geometries' as well as other forms of visual design. We might sense it when we engage with paintings, film and any of nature's beautiful objects, but it's also what we feel when we see a Mayan pyramid or the magnificent boulevards in Paris. Research has also found that art has the possibility of an impact beyond awe. The more people engage in art, the more committed they are to their communities and the more creative they are.

6. Spiritual and religious awe

Religious and spiritual practices intentionally incorporate awe-inspiring elements on several levels. We might experience this in the architecture of the temples, churches or mosques in which people gather, but it's also evident in the rituals and ceremonies designed to connect the faithful with the transcendent or divine. Like all experiences of awe, those encountered in a religious or spiritual context can awaken a sense of humility, reverence and connection to a higher power or the universe. In these settings, awe can serve as a bridge between the individual and the sacred, offering a pathway to spiritual and moral growth. By engaging with the awe-inspiring aspects of our faith or spirituality, we can cultivate a deeper sense of interconnectedness with those around us and also with life's greater meaning.

7. Stories of birth and death

In each of the 26 cultural groups studied by Keltner, people shared stories of experiencing moments of transcendence when bearing witness to the beginning or end of a life. There's nothing quite as awe-invoking as the moment a baby arrives in the world and maybe nothing quite as profound as the experience of being with someone as they take their last breath.

8. Epiphanies

Moments of sudden insight or realisation can be deeply awe-inspiring because they often involve a profound shift in perspective or understanding. The epiphanies we experience might come about from philosophical insights, metaphysical ideas or mathematic equations but, equally, they may be felt as personal realisations. These can open our minds to new possibilities, reveal hidden truths or provide us with a sense of clarity that transcends our ordinary experience. Such moments of insight remind us of the vastness of human potential and can expand our understanding of the world and our place within it.

Exploring spirituality

Dr Lisa Miller, professor and researcher at Columbia University, believes that spirituality is not merely an abstract concept but a tangible factor that plays a significant role in mental and emotional wellbeing.

One of the standout findings from her studies is the correlation between spirituality and resilience. Individuals with a strong spiritual foundation tend to navigate life's challenges with greater ease, viewing them as opportunities for growth rather than insurmountable obstacles. Spiritual engagement can also act as a protective factor against depression and provide us with a greater sense of belonging and purpose.

Spirituality can be accessed in small ways. When practised regularly, these habits can bring you a sense of peace, perspective and belonging.

Embrace ritual at the start of your day

Create a morning ritual that will help you interact with your day in a more conscious way. Choose a small daily action such as a meditating upon waking, practising a few sun salutations, adopting a gratitude practice or engaging in reflective writing.

Set an intention for the day

Reflect on the day ahead and create a mental picture of the person you'd like to be in your day. Consider the interactions you'll have and ask yourself how you might make a difference to the people you'll encounter in your day.

Create the right physical spaces

If you're living or working in a building that seems to be depleting your energy, take notice of this. It's likely that you're not imagining it. If there's a strong negative feeling associated with one of these spaces, consider what you can change about it. Try diffusing essential oils or using a space-clearing spray (or if you're more open-minded, try 'smudging' the space with palo santo or sage). Include personal items in your workspace if possible or talk to a feng shui consultant about remedies such as adding colour or a wind chime to help shift the energy.

Keep your own energy healthy

Start by implementing small amounts of change such as eating more plant-based foods and drinking herbal teas rather than too much alcohol or caffeine. Move your body in ways that feel supportive and nourishing rather than pushing yourself to do harsh forms of exercise. Meditate, practise yoga, qigong or Pilates, swim in the ocean, have a massage or try energy healing.

Stay connected to nature

In a Japanese study on the benefits of forest bathing, researchers found that 'forest air doesn't just feel fresher and better – inhaling phytoncide seems to actually improve immune system function'. Find a place to walk among the trees or connect with the healing powers of the sea by walking barefoot along the beach. Spend an afternoon in mineral hot springs, swim in the ocean or take yourself to your local public gardens and spend 30 minutes lying on the grass.

Explore your own version of spirituality

Dive into spiritual texts, attend workshops, or engage in discussions to explore different aspects of spirituality. Continuous exploration and understanding of different philosophies can enrich your own experience of spirituality.

Bringing it all together: Annabelle's story

When Annabelle came to see me, she had lost not only her confidence but also her marriage, her job, many of her friends, her home, her car and her savings. This downward spiral had begun just before the global pandemic. A few months after giving birth to her little boy, Annabelle discovered that her husband had been lying to her, not only about the dire state of their finances but also about his 'late nights at the office', which he'd spent sleeping with one of his colleagues.

Annabelle felt like the man she had known for seven years had suddenly become a complete stranger – he wasn't even showing interest in the baby boy he'd wanted so badly. Exhausted from sleepless nights and navigating parenthood alone, Annabelle felt overwhelmed by the choices she faced but was clear about one thing: she couldn't stay in this marriage and spend the rest of her life waiting to be deceived again.

When Annabelle and her husband separated, she spent the first few months in shock, just going through the motions of mothering. She began to negotiate divorce proceedings and in doing so discovered the true state of their financial affairs just as the world was hit by the pandemic and things got significantly worse.

By the time she came to see me, her little boy was four and she was only just beginning to explore how to heal. She was contemplating putting herself back out into the world to rebuild friendships and find new work, but told me that her confidence was (understandably) at an all-time low. We decided to focus first on helping her to rediscover her sense of self.

For Annabelle, this process began with her reconnecting with an earlier love of yoga. Tuning in to her body gave her the awareness to notice and name her emotions. She began to let herself grieve for all that she had lost, and over time, she learned to be more present and accepting of her sadness and fear. She read Lisa Miller's book, *The Awakened Brain*, and told me that she found great comfort in connecting with the spiritual teachings at her yoga school. Eventually, she decided she would work with others who had been through similar experiences to her, giving her work a renewed sense of meaning and purpose.

Her greatest accomplishment, in my opinion, was learning to find her way back to presence each time she interacted with her ex-husband – something she found anxiety-provoking and confronting. When she noticed herself feeling fear or the inclination to be submissive, she used breathing exercises to bring her back to centre and remind her of her inner strength and courage.

By becoming more grounded and centred, Annabelle experienced a radical shift in the dynamic of her relationship with her ex-husband. She no longer felt powerless, and was much more confident when it came to advocating for her son, which gave all of her experience more meaning.

While you now have a roadmap to quiet confidence, the pathway to achieving it is rarely linear and it's likely that there'll be obstacles and setbacks along the way. If you find yourself doubting your choices, your values will guide you back to what's important to you. When you're feeling critical of yourself, remind yourself of your strengths and connect to the confident part of yourself to help quieten those worrying thoughts.

On the days that you make a mistake or encounter criticism from someone else, find your way back to self-compassion, by writing a letter of kindness to yourself or simply reminding yourself that you're human and you don't need to do everything perfectly.

And keep in mind Kent Hoffman's words, that *every person has infinite worth*. You matter, even when you're being imperfect.

TWENTY-ONE

Embracing imperfection

Making peace with imperfection isn't about lowering your standards but recognising that being human means you're going to make mistakes, and that growth can arise from the inevitable errors and challenges we all face.

We also need to recognise that the very idea of 'perfection' is a construct. What one person deems perfect, another might see as somehow flawed. More importantly, the quest for perfection is a moving target. Achieving one perfect milestone inevitably leads to the creation of another. This cycle can become exhausting, leaving us perpetually dissatisfied and always striving for the next best thing.

When we shed the mask of perfection and the illusion that perfection is achievable, we can give up the internal goal of wanting or needing to be perfect. In doing so, we give ourselves permission to present our genuine selves to the world. As so much of the research shows, this authenticity fosters a deeper connection with ourselves and others and allows us to be truly seen and appreciated for who we are, which are foundational elements of presence.

Keep coming back to the middle of the river

The River of Integration metaphor, which we introduced earlier in the book, serves as a helpful representation of the mental and emotional states we often navigate as we work our way towards confidence. On one side of the river, there's the bank of chaos, where emotions and thoughts whirl without structure, leading to feelings of being overwhelmed, anxious or disoriented. On the opposite side lies the bank of rigidity, a realm of excessive control, inflexibility and resistance to change.

In the same way that those banks represent chaos and control, we might think of them as representing any of the polarities we experience in life and, in particular, those we encounter on our journey to confidence. One bank might represent over-confidence and the other, extreme self-doubt. One could be striving and the other, complacency.

It's helpful to remember that neither bank is a favourable place. The true magic lies in the 'glorious middle' of the river itself – the place where we can arrive at a state of integration where we balance fluidity and structure. It's in the central flow that we find mental harmony, emotional resilience and the capacity to respond to life's challenges with flexibility and composure.

Being in this river means we allow ourselves to fully experience all of our emotions, and we can process them and let them pass without becoming overwhelmed or trying to suppress them.

We don't try to fight against the flow of the river. Instead, we work with the current while keeping an eye on the distance (and our most meaningful goals), moving back towards the centre at every opportunity.

Mindfulness is a tool that can be used to help us to achieve integration. By being present and attuned to our inner experiences, we come to recognise when we're veering too close to either bank and we can gently guide ourselves back to balance.

It's from this balanced place that we can remind ourselves that each of us, by the sheer fact of our existence, has inherent value. This intrinsic worth isn't contingent upon our achievements, societal validation, or by the comparisons we make between ourselves and other people. Acknowledging and embracing this can be a foundational step in fostering genuine self-worth.

Our cultural narratives frequently celebrate success, happiness and comfort while devaluing failure, sadness and discomfort, but self-worth comes from accepting the entirety of our experience. This means embracing our vulnerabilities, imperfections and uncertainties just as we do our strengths, achievements and certainties.

Many years ago, I had a conversation with Robert Rabbin, a wise mentor and greatly valued friend who has now passed. Robert's view of the world was that there is no hierarchy. 'The way we view success,' he told me, 'is inherently flawed.' We measure people by the positions they hold, by their intellect and appearance, by the possessions they own, as well as other outward measures of supposed success.

Robert's view was that instead of subscribing to this vertical view of hierarchy (the CEO at the top and the most junior worker at the bottom of the ladder), we need to tilt the vertical ladder until it's horizontal and recognise that along this axis, each of us inhabits our own unique and valuable place.

Rather than resisting or avoiding the discomfort that accompanies our flaws, maybe the deepest signifier of quiet confidence is trusting that we can lean into *everything* that we are. By consciously engaging with our fears, anxieties, and the memories of things we wish we could change, we cultivate resilience and a deeper appreciation for our growth and our strengths.

Grounding ourselves in the present moment is the pathway to recognising the inherent sense of freedom and self-worth that is possible when we accept ourselves, just as we are. By letting go of past regrets and future anxieties and immersing ourselves in the 'now', we can experience life more authentically.

Engaging in a loving, compassionate dialogue with yourself, especially during moments of doubt, will fortify feelings of self-worth.

Within life's dualities, there lies an opportunity for profound acceptance and peace. As we navigate the path to quiet confidence, armed with the wisdom of many great teachers, we uncover the treasure that has always been with us: our unparalleled, unwavering and innate sense of worthiness. It's from this place of worth that quiet confidence grows and radiates. When we can strengthen our connection to this through the many small ways we've explored in this book, it's a reminder that it is our unique collection of strengths, characteristics and life experiences that makes each of us a rare and unpolished gem.

Presence summary

- The three pillars of executive presence are gravitas, communication and a minor focus on grooming and appearance.
- Having 'presence' involves being able to be more 'present'. Practise coming back to the present moment by learning meditation, mindful movement, focusing on your breath, learning to centre yourself and be grounded.
- 'Awe' describes the feeling of being connected to something bigger than ourselves. This feeling can help us create perspective, foster unity and purpose, and connect us with the source of energy within.
- Research suggests we find awe in the following places: moral beauty, collective effervescence, nature, music, visual design, spiritual and religious experiences, stories of birth and death, and epiphanies.
- As we continue our journey to confidence, we need to remind ourselves that the pathway will continue to be imperfect.
- Between life's dualities, there's an opportunity for profound acceptance and peace.

Acknowledgements

Firstly, a big thank you to Susan Cain for your brilliant book, *Quiet: The Power of Introverts in a World That Can't Stop Talking*. It changed so much for me. Your work, your humility and your authenticity have been a great source of inspiration.

Thanks to the incredibly talented Katie Bosher for collaborating on this book. Our conversations, your research and your brilliant way of helping me to clarify my ideas have made a real difference.

Thank you again to the fabulous team at Pan Macmillan and in particular, Ingrid Ohlsson for allowing me to write the book that feels most meaningful to me.

Thank you to Rebecca Lay, Brianne Collins, Ariane Durkin and Danielle Walker for your wonderful editing skills. Thanks to Candice Wyman and Charlotte Ree for getting the book out into the world and to Grace Carter, Candace Chidiac and Sally Devenish for keeping things humming away in the background.

A big thank you to Lisa White for the beautiful the cover design.

Thanks to the incredible writers and researchers whose wisdom inspires and informs the way that I work with my clients. Special thanks to Zach Mercurio, Dacher Keltner, Alain de Botton, Dr Lisa Miller, Dr Rebecca Ray, Elizabeth Gilbert, Katty Kay, Claire Shipman, James Clear, Dr Carrie Hayward, Dr Daniel Siegel and Amy Cuddy.

Thank you to the dear friends who are a continued source of support and encouragement – Barb Long, Meredith Monti, Deb Boyce, Karen Ramaekers, Lindy Lloyd, Glenis Dennison, Catherine Morey-Nase, Onny Aivatoglou, Jane Barrett and Jackie Power.

Thank you to the wonderful experts who so generously shared their time and wisdom in my online program, *The Confidence Course* – Catherine Morey-Nase, Carrie Hayward, Nina Perry, Lisa Stockman, Sarah Denholm, Julie Ta, Belinda Winter and Jodi Wilson.

The biggest thank you to Chris for taking such great care of our home, our garden and me, not just while I write, but always. It's hard to believe we've spent almost 40 years together – it never seems long enough.

Enormous thanks to my daughters Elsa and Meg for your belief in me, for reminding me to laugh, for the abundance of love and support, and for being such inspiring role models of quiet confidence.

Thanks to Toby and our darling grandchildren, Oscar and Milla for being a constant source of joy. We can't wait to meet 'baby sister' who is due to arrive at pretty much the same time as this book is released.

And finally, a huge thank you to every one of my incredible clients who have taught me more about the human condition, humility, confidence and compassion than all the books I've read. It is a privilege to work with you.

Endnotes

Introduction

4. Introverts make up as much as 30 to 50 per cent of the world's population . . . .: Jenn Granneman, 'There might not be as many extroverts in the world as we think, science says', *Introvert, Dear*, 9 April 2015, www. introvertdear.com; Jenna Goudreau, 'So Begins A Quiet Revolution Of The 50 Percent', *Forbes*, 30 January 2012, www.forbes.com; Melissa Summer, 'Introverts and Leadership – World Introvert Day', *The Myers-Briggs Company*, 2 January 2020, www.themyersbriggs.com

11. Their original study involved testing people on grammar, humour and logic . . .: Justin Kruger and David Dunning, 'Unskilled and unaware of it: How difficulties in recognizing one's own incompetence lead to inflated self-assessments', *Journal of Personality and Social Psychology*, vol. 77, no. 6, December 1999, pp. 1121–1134.

13. It's also the case in corporate America . . .: Kate Ludeman and Eddie Erlandson, 'Coaching the alpha male', *Harvard Business Review*, May 2004, [Accessed May 2023], www.hbr.com

15. Susan Cain says that 'knowing things isn't enough . . .': Susan Cain, *Quiet: The Power of Introverts in a World That Can't Stop Talking*, Viking, Penguin Group, 2012.

16. In a series of tests, hundreds of university students . . .: Katty Kay and Claire Shipman, *The Confidence Code: The Science and Art of*

Self-Assurance—What Women Should Know, HarperCollins Publishers Australia, 2014 (Epub).

16. Despite this, women around the world are paid 17 per cent less than men . . .: Katherine Haan, 'Gender pay gap statistics in 2023', *Forbes Advisor*, February 2023, www.forbes.com

16. . . . and only 10 per cent of Fortune 500 companies globally are run by women: Emma Hinchliffe, 'Women CEOs run 10.4% of Fortune 500 Companies. A quarter of the 52 leaders became CEO in the last year', *Fortune*, June 2023, www.fortune.com

16. Many studies have shown that when women make money and lead companies . . .: Angie O'Leary, 'When women control the wealth, society reap the benefits', *MarketWatch*, April 2019, www.marketwatch.com

18. In *The Myth of Normal,* renowned Canadian physician and author Gabor Maté . . .: Joanna Cheek, MD, 'Smiling to Death: The hidden dangers of being "nice"', *Psychology Today*, 20 April 2023, www.psychologytoday.com

20. Talented women judge themselves more harshly than men . . .: Katherine Handcock, 'Why bright girls struggle: When ability doesn't lead to confidence', *A Mighty Girl*, 17 August 2023, www.amightygirl.com

25. The test they developed is still widely used around the world . . .: www.16personalities.com

28. And just fifty years later, this definition . . .: *Online Etymology Dictionary*, www.etymonline.com

29. The cultures of Sweden, Denmark and Finland, for example . . .: Darcy Jacobsen, 'Recognizing Across Cultures: Scandinavia', *Workhuman*, 1 August 2015, www.workhuman.com

29. Though each is very different, the cultures of these countries . . .: Cain, op. cit.

29. The Chinese word *wu wei* describes . . .: Whitney Johnson, 'Lead without trying so hard', *Harvard Business Review*, 16 July 2014, www.hbr.org

30. A leader who embraces *wu wei* . . .: Laurent Auzoult, 'Wu wei: A contribution to the water-like leadership style', *Journal of Management Spirituality & Religion*, vol. 18, no. 4, June 2021, pp. 312–331.

30. In South Korea, the twin phenomena of *jeong* and *woori* . . .: Hai Kyong Kim et al, 'How Korean Leadership style cultivates employees' creativity and voice in hierarchical organizations', *SAGE Open*, vol. 9, no. 3, 2019. doi.org/10.1177/2158244019876281

33. The industrial revolution had a dramatic effect . . .: Cain, op. cit.

36. During a class at graduate school, a professor of Kent's . . .: Kent Hoffman, *Every Person Has Infinite Worth*, TED speech, TEDxSpokane, 26 November 2015

38. Today, he spreads the message . . .: ibid.

42. When we believe we are less worthy than others . . .: Dr Rajiv Jhangiani, Dr Hammond Tarry and Dr Charles Stangor, *Principles of Social Psychology: 1st International H5P Edition*, BCampus, Canada, 2022.

42. A more helpful view of self-esteem . . .: Dr Melanie Fennell, *Overcoming Low Self-Esteem: A self-help guide using cognitive behavioural techniques*, Robinson, 2016.

44. Other experts point to the more accepted theory . . .: Kay and Shipman, op. cit.

45. It seems our genes influence everything . . .: ibid.

45. As powerful as nature is, scientists now believe . . .: ibid.

49. Any decisions we make from this place . . .: Scott Orth, 'Living life between chaos and rigidity', *Mindful Wisdom*, 2016, [Accessed 1 June 2023], www.mindfulwisdom.ca

52. We feel safest when things are familiar . . .: Dr Robert Maurer, PhD, *Spirit of Kaizen: Creating lasting excellence one small step at a time*, McGraw Hill, November 2012; Robert Maurer, PhD, *One Small Step Can Change Your Life*, Thomas Allen & Son Limited, Canada, 2014.

54. There is beauty in small, consistent changes . . .: Matthew Pollard with Derek Lewis, *The Introverts Edge: How the quiet and shy can outsell anyone*, AMACOM, (Epub) 1st edition, 2018.

56. Compassion is best described as . . .: Jennifer Goetz et al, 'Compassion: An evolutionary analysis and empirical review', *Psychological Bulletin*, vol. 136, no. 3, May 2010, pp. 351–374.

59. Research suggests that physical touch helps to release oxytocin . . .: Kristin Neff, 'Exercise 4: Supportive touch', *Self-Compassion*, www.self-compassion.org

Part One: Meaning

65. I reassured her that while seeking meaning might seem idealistic to some people . . .: Martin Seligman, *Authentic Happiness*, Simon & Schuster, New York, 2004.

68. Another thing the religious world has done far more effectively . . .: *The Agenda with Steve Paikin*, television interview, TVO Today, Toronto, 2012 [Accessed via TVO YouTube June 2023].

68. Someone who self-identifies as having a meaningful spiritual life . . .: Rachel Martin, 'This ivy-league researcher says spirituality is good for our mental health', *NPR*, July 2023, www.npr.org; Lois Collins, 'Finding the light: The science behind spirituality as an anti-depressant', *Deseret News,* December 2022, www.deseret.com

69. Over time, they formed a new ritual: Melissa Cunningham, 'The Sea Wolves: Cold-water swimming helps women find healing and friendship', *The Age*, April 2023, www.theage.com.au

72. While they are an important part of life . . .: Elizabeth Scott, PhD, 'Hedonic Adaptation: Why you are not happier', *Verywell Mind,* June 2022, www.verywellmind.com

74. American troops noticed a similar pattern of behaviour . . .: Viktor E. Frankl, *Man's Search for Meaning*, Beacon Press, Boston, 2006.

74. We have freedom to find meaning . . .: Maria Marshall and Edward Marshall, *Logotherapy Revisited: Review of the Tenets of Viktor E. Frankl's Logotherapy*, Ottawa Institute of Logotherapy, Ottawa 2012. ISBN 978-1-4781–9377–7.OCLC 1100192135. [Accessed 6 July 2023].

80. According to Stanford professor Kelly McGonigal, writing about your values . . .: Kelly McGonigal, *The Upside of Stress: Why stress is good for you, and how to get good at it,* Avery Publishing Group, 2016.

92. According to a 2015 study, those who write their goals down . . .: Marie Forleo, 'Self-made millionaire: The simple strategy that helped me increase my odds of success by 42%', CNBC *Make It,* September 2019, www.cnbc.com; Sarah Gardner and Dave Albee, *Study Focuses on Strategies for Achieving Goals, Resolutions*, media release, Dominican University of California, California, February 2015.

92. One of the reasons for this is that the action of writing . . .: Mark Murphy, 'Neuroscience explains why you need to write down your goals if you actually want to achieve them', *Forbes*, April 2018, www.forbes.com

93. The likelihood of achieving a goal jumps to 62 per cent . . .: Dominican University of California, Goals Research Summary, www.dominican.edu

99. Write your life story in the third person . . .: Courtney E. Ackerman, MA, '19 best narrative therapy techniques and worksheets', *Positive Psychology.com,* June 2017, www.positivepsychology.com

100. In a discussion with Pico Iyer . . .: 'The future of hope', *On Being,* podcast, 18 November 2021.

101. Though we may never be able to say we are glad for those experiences . . .: ibid.

101. As we do this, we may come to appreciate paradoxes . . .: Sivan S. Aulov et al, 'Posttraumatic growth', *Encyclopedia of Mental Health (Third Edition)*, vol. 2, 2023.

102. Your ability to move forward from adversity . . .: 'Post-traumatic growth', *Psychology Today*, www.psychologytoday.com

109. Héctor García, co-author of the book *Ikigai* . . .: 'The secret to a joyful life', *The Government of Japan*, March 2022, www.japan.g.jp

109. 'When we asked what their *ikigai* was . . .': ibid.

111. For the past decade, he's been studying what gives our lives purpose and meaning . . .: Zach Mercurio, PhD, 'Why "find your purpose" is terrible advice', *Medium*, June 2016, www.medium.com

114. 'Now, for the first time, I saw the real effects of being shoeless . . .': Blake Mycoskie, 'How I did it: The TOMS story', *Entrepreneur*, September 2011, www.entrepreneur.com

115. 'From the beginning, she realised that . . .': ibid.

116. They've helped millions of people in need . . .: TOMS, 'Blake Mycoskie, TOMS founder', 2023, www.TOMS.com

Part Two: Connection

124. According to Dr Michelle McQuaid . . .: Michelle McQuaid, PhD, '10 Reasons to Focus on Your Strengths', *Psychology Today*, November 2014, www.psychologytoday.com

125. The overwhelming majority believed we needed to focus . . .: Marcus Buckingham, 'How to Stop Fixating on Failure', *Marcus Buckingham*, 19 June 2019, www.marcusbuckingham.com

125. The best leaders in the world understand that *strengths* . . .: ibid.

125. The leaders' job was to define the role . . .: 'Harnessing Your Strengths', *Young and Profiting*, podcast, March 2021, ep. 104.

126. In research spanning six different studies . . .: Andreas Steimer and André Mata, 'Motivated Implicit Theories of Personality: My Weaknesses Will Go Away, but My Strengths Are Here to Stay', *Personality and Social Psychology Bulletin*, vol. 42, no. 4, 16 March 2016.

127. The excellent news for all of us, is . . .: Jessica Greene, 'Work on your strengths, not your weaknesses', *Zapier*, 9 May 2019, www.zapier.com

127. 'Research shows that extroverts process information faster than introverts' . . .: Carly Breit, 'The surprising benefits of being an introvert', *TIME*, 27 August 2018, www.time.com

129. An article on the website *Introvert, Dear,* points to seven key advantages . . .: Jetta Moon, '7 distinct advantages introverts have over extroverts', *Introvert, Dear,* December 2020, www.introvertdear.com

131. Being highly sensitive is an innate personality trait . . .: Elaine N. Aron, PhD, *The Highly Sensitive Person,* 2023, www.hsperson.com

131. Just like introversion, being an HSP . . .: '10 Strengths of a highly sensitive person & weaknesses', *High 5 Test,* 2023, www.high5test.com

132. Free online assessments such as the one specifically for HSPs . . .: ibid.

133. Before you complete the other profiling tools . . .: Alex Linley, *Average To A+: Realising strengths in yourself and others,* CAPP Press, 2008.

134. On the VIA Signature Strengths website . . .: www.viacharacter.org

134. Author Sally Kempton writes about another concept I love . . .: Sally Kempton, 'Me and my shadow', *Sally Kempton,* 2 September 2019, www.sallykempton.com

137. When Martin Seligman and 24 other researchers . . .: Martin Seligman, *Flourish: A visionary new understanding of happiness and well-being,* Atria Books, reprint edition, 2012.

145. This voice is what I would call her wise, knowing, confident self: 'Creativity & Internal Family Systems', *All Parts Welcome,* podcast, ep. 1, 23 May 2023.

145. Sinking into a pile of clothes in her closet, she challenged herself . . .: Glennon Doyle, *Untamed: Stop pleasing, start living,* Vermillion, London, 2020, pp. 57–58.

145. This innately confident aspect of ourselves . . .: Richard C. Schwartz, PhD, *No Bad Parts: Healing trauma and restoring wholeness with the Internal Family Systems Model,* Sounds True, Colorado, 2021.

146. It typically shows up as a 'feeling' . . .: Simone Wright, 'The 4 levels of intuition: Recognizing the voice of your highest wisdom', *Huffpost,* October 2014, www.huffpost.com

146. Many people report that this sensation comes from their belly area . . .: 'The brain-gut connection', *Johns Hopkins Medicine,* 2023, www.hopkinsmedicine.org

150. This brief transition between wakefulness and sleep . . .: Allison Eck, 'Behind the veil of hypnagogic sleep', *Harvard Medicine,* Autumn 2022, www.magazine.hms.harvard.edu

153. *Do I contradict myself?. . .: A Song of Myself,* Walt Whitman, 1850.

153. Mainstream religions also supported this theory . . .: Schwartz, op. cit.

154. The subversive idea that the mind is naturally multiple . . .: *Greater than the sum of our parts*, Insights at the Edge Podcast, Sounds True, 17 July 2018, [Accessed July 2023].

155. He came to believe that what we generally call *thinking* . . .: *No Bad Parts*, Insights at the Edge Podcast, Sounds True, 22 June 2021, [Accessed July 2023].

155. By working *with* instead of against these critical voices . . .: Schwartz, op. cit.

156. The goal of IFS isn't to eliminate the difficult parts . . .: *Greater Than the Sum of Our Parts,* op. cit.

157. And although they mean well, the impact they can have . . .: Schwartz, *No Bad Parts*, op. cit.

157. It is an innate force that is within all of us . . .: ibid.

159. It's rooted in a primal part of ourselves . . .: Jasbinder Garnermann, 'The Origin of the Shadow', *Jung Centre*, 2017, www.jungcentre.com

160. If we aren't aware of these shadow selves . . .: Sally Kempton, 'Me and My Shadow', *Sally Kempton*, September 2019, www.sallykempton.com

160. Interestingly, our shadow selves are usually . . .: ibid.

160. Behind it is where her authentic self and shadow self hide . . .: Kendra Cherry, MSEd, 'What are the Jungian Archetypes?', *Very WellMind*, March 2023, www.verywellmind.com

161. These exercises might be uncomfortable initially . . .: ibid.

166. Instead, it's about helping them to transition . . .: IFS Institute, *The Internal Family Systems Model Outline*, 2023, www.ifs-institute.com

169. In 2019, researchers examining the results of 52 studies . . .: American Psychological Association, *Positive Relationships Boost Self-esteem, and vice versa*, September 2019, www.apa.org

170. 'If you get sick or a spouse dies, or if you run out of money . . .': Aislinn Kotifani, 'Moai: This tradition is why Okinawan people live longer, better', *Blue Zones*, August 2018, www.bluezones.com

170. This incredible social safety net offers the security . . .: Susan Pinker, *The Secret to Living Longer May Be Your Social Life*, *TED*, April 2017, www.TED.com

172. Social connection has more to do with our *subjective* feeling of connection . . .: Emma Seppala, Timothy Rossomando and James R. Doty, 'Social Connection and Compassion: Important Predictors of Health and Well-Being', *Social Research*, vol. 80, no. 2, Summer 2013, pp. 411–430.

173. In a series of studies that looked at the lifestyles . . . .: Julianne Holt-Lunstad et al, 'Social relationships and mortality risk: A meta-analytic review', *PLOS* Medicine, vol. 7, no. 7, e1000316, 27 July 2010.

175. In 2019, after data revealed that . . . .: Dutch News, *Jumbo opens 'chat checkouts' to combat loneliness among the elderly*, 28 September 2021, www.dutchnews.nl; Cathryn Boyes, 'Supermarket opens chat checkouts to combat loneliness', *The New Daily*, 12 October 2021, www.thenewdaily.com.au

176. Loneliness affects introverts just as much as extroverts . . . .: Laurie Helgoe, PhD, *Introvert Power: Why your inner life is your hidden strength*, Sourcebooks, Inc., Naperville, Illinois, (second edition) February 2013.

178. Dr Gordon Flett, who researches and writes about mattering . . . .: Sally Manninen interview with Dr Gordon Flett, 'The Power of Mattering', *Choose To Be Healthy*, 26 May 2022, www.YouTube.com

179. Researchers have also discovered that mattering . . . .: ibid.

179. 'When someone doesn't believe they matter at work . . . .: Zach Mercurio, 'How to create mattering at work', *Zach Mercurio*, 15 November 2022, www.zachmercurio.com

180. Luke's experience reflects the findings of a 2023 study . . . .: Nathan Morris, 'Ending loneliness together report finds almost 33 pc [sic] of Australians feel lonely and disconnected', *ABC News*, 7 August 2023, www.abc.net.au

186. We need to have face-to-face contact . . . .: Pinker, op. cit.

Part Three: Courage

189. If anything, it's very likely to sap it: Randy A. Sansone, MD, and Lori A. Sansone, MD, 'Rumination: Relationships with physical health', *Innovations in Clinical Neuroscience*, vol. 9, no. 2, February 2012, pp. 29–34.

189. In the first part of this book, I wrote about the study . . . .: Kay and Shipman, op. cit.

193. The word 'courage' comes from the Latin word *cor* (heart) . . . .: Brené Brown, *I Thought It Was Just Me: Women reclaiming power and courage in a culture of shame*, Penguin Books, 2011.

193. Speaking from the heart is what Brené Brown . . . .: ibid.

199. Recent research suggests that introverts are . . . .: Kevin Wood, 'Introverts in conflict: what we learned in 2022', *The Myers-Briggs Company*, 2 January 2023, www.themyersbriggs.com

214. When we do this, we become less swayed by external validation . . .:
Tara Mohr, *Playing Big: Find Your Voice, Your Mission, Your Message,*
Penguin Books, 2014.

217. It took Charles Darwin 34 years to publish his theory . . .: Susan Cain,
'How to overcome the fear of "Putting yourself out there"', *The Kindred
Letters* (Newsletter), 13 July 2023.

217. If you find the thought of sharing your ideas . . .: ibid.

222. For a long time, the two main responses were fight and flight . . .: Kelly
Burch, 'How you react to stressful situations explains a lot about you,
your personality and circumstances', *Business Insider NL*, 8 December
2022, www.buisnessinsider.nl

223. Bulleted list in Fight: Knotted stomach/nausea, burning stomach . . .:
Human Relations Institute & Clinics, *Trauma Response: The 4 F's –
Fight, flight, freeze, and fawn*, 2023, www.hricdubai.com

223. Bulleted list in Flight: Reported or observed fidgety-ness, restlessness,
feeling trapped . . .: ibid.

223–4. Bulleted list in Freeze ending in Decreased heart rate (although can
sometimes increase) . . .: ibid.

224. Bulleted list in Fawn: Pretending to agree with others . . .: ibid.

226. Professor Sarah Gershman teaches public speaking to leaders . . .:
Sarah Gershman, 'To overcome your fear of public speaking, stop
thinking about yourself', *Harvard Business Review*, 17 September 2019,
[Accessed September 2023], www.hbr.org

228. And if you couldn't get rid of it . . .: Elizabeth Gilbert, 'Facing fear
with self-compassion', *Insight Timer*, 2021, www.insighttimer.com

228. The turning point came for Liz . . .: ibid.

229. When she's scared, nervous or daunted . . .: ibid.

231. Think, *If the most loving, supportive and strong person . . .*: ibid.

233. An impressive 11.15 million viewers in Australia . . .: Marita Moloney,
'World Cup: Matildas score TV rating record in semi-final loss to
England', *BBC*, 17 August 2023, [Accessed September 2023], www.
bbc.com

235. In 2010, Eric 'Astro' Teller – head of Google X, the company's secret
laboratory . . .: David Grossman, 'Secret Google lab "rewards staff for
failure"', *BBC*, 24 January 2014. [Accessed September 2023], www.
bbc.com

237. A poll of 750 executive women in the US revealed . . .: KPMG,
*Advancing the Future of Women in Business: The 2020 KPMG Women's
Leadership Summit Report*, October 2020.

238. In her book, *Presence*, Cuddy says that . . .: Shana Lebowitz, 'Men are suffering from a psychological phenomenon that can undermine their success, but they're too ashamed to talk about it', *Business Insider*, 13 January 2016. [Accessed 10 September 2023], www.businessinsider.com

238. As Atlassian grew from a two-man start-up . . .: Mike Cannon-Brookes, 'How to use your imposter syndrome as an asset', *Inside Atlassian*, 3 December 2018, www.atlassian.com

239. Imposter syndrome was clearly something that everybody deals with . . .: Mike Cannon-Brookes, *How you can use imposter syndrome to your benefit, TED*, TEDxSydney, July 2017. www.TED.com

241. Women also pointed to having . . .: Paulsie, op. cit.

242. Being selected had also added more pressure to perform . . .: Marnee Vinall, 'Do I belong here?: The young Matilda struggling with imposter syndrome', *Sydney Morning Herald*, 4 July 2023, [Accessed 16 September 2023], www.smh.com.au

242. One of these is a tattoo . . .: ibid.

242. 'If we can encourage young girls to get into football . . .': ibid.

Part Four: Presence

251. 'There is a middle path but it goes only one direction . . .': Cheryl Strayed, *Tiny Beautiful Things: Advice on Love and Life from Dear Sugar*, Vintage Books, 2012.

254. A 2018 study of corporate leaders found . . .: Sylvia Ann Hewlett et al, *Executive Presence: Key findings*, COQUAL (formerly Center for Talent Innovation), 2013, www.coqual.org

259. In her book *Presence*, Amy Cuddy describes true presence . . .: Amy Cuddy, *Presence: Bringing your boldest self to your biggest challenges*, Orion, London, 2015.

260. It also makes us more inclined to . . .: ibid.

261. These habits are all done unconsciously . . .: Howard Allen, 'Self Adaptors, Alter Adaptors and Object Adaptors in Nonverbal Communication', 27 April 2019, www. owlcation.com

261. Women frequently undermine themselves . . .: Tara Mohr, '8 Ways Women Undermine Themselves with Their Words', www.taramohr.com

271. These studies have been small in scale . . .: James L. Oschman et al, 'The effects of grounding (earthing) on inflammation, the immune

response, wound healing, and prevention and treatment of chronic inflammatory and autoimmune diseases', *Journal of Inflammation Research*, vol. 8, 24 March 2015, pp. 83–96.

271. . . . improve sleep and reduce stress: M. Ghaly and D. Teplitz, 'The biologic effects of grounding the human body during sleep as measured by cortisol levels and subjective reporting of sleep, pain, and stress', *Journal of Alternative and Complementary Medicine*, vol. 10, no. 5, 2004, pp. 767–776.

271. It is also believed to increase energy . . .: Gaétan Chevalier, 'The effect of grounding the human body on mood', *Psychological Reports*, vol. 116, no. 2, April 2015, pp. 496–514.

274. Awe does more than just give us goosebumps . . .: Dacher Keltner, *Awe: The Transformative Power of Wonder*, Penguin Random House, UK, 2023.

274. One study also found that awe . . .: Summer Allen, PhD, *The Science of Awe: A white paper prepared for the John Templeton Foundation*, Greater Good Science Center at UC Berkeley, September 2018, www.ggsc. berkeley.edu

274. It can help us to focus less on the default self . . .: Keltner, op. cit.

275. Awe can increase our feelings of connectedness . . .: Allen, op. cit.

275. Researchers believed that recalling awe . . .: Melanie Rudd et al, 'Awe Expands People's Perception of Time, Alters Decision Making, and Enhances Well-Being', *Psychological Science*, vol. 23, no. 10, 1 October 2012, pp. 1130–1136.

277. But we're just as likely to find . . .: Keltner, op. cit.

278. Research has also found that art . . .: The Overview, *Dr. Dacher Keltner: How art opens our eyes to everyday awe*, 6 May 2023, www.theoverview. art

278. The more people engage in art . . .: Greater Good In Education (UC Berkeley), *Finding Awe in Visual Design*, 2023, www.ggie.berkeley.edu

281. In a Japanese study on the benefits of forest bathing . . .: Ephrat Livni, 'The Japanese practice of "forest bathing" is scientifically proven to improve your health', *Quartz*, 12 October 2016, www.qz.com